New South Wales Mathematics Syllabus

New Syllabus MENTALS and Extension

Paul Nightingale

STAGE ONE
BOOK 2

A
FIVE SENSES
PUBLICATION

A
FIVE SENSES PUBLICATION

Copyright © 2022 Paul Nightingale - Five Senses Education Pty. Ltd.
New Syllabus Mentals and Extension - Stage One Book 2

Published by:
Five Senses Education Pty Ltd.
ABN: 16 001 414 437
2/195 Prospect Highway Seven Hills NSW 2147
Ph: 02 9838 9265
email: sevenhills@fivesenseseducation.com.au
website: www.fivesenseseducation.com.au

Cover Design: Brooke Lewis

National Library of Australia Card No.
and ISBN 978-1-76032-403-2

About this Book for the Teacher

New South Wales Mathematics K-2 Syllabus has been developed to help raise the standard of mathematics in the first three years of formal schooling. This book, *New Syllabus Mentals and Extension Book 2* reinforces and extends the activities introduced in *New Syllabus Maths, Stage One Book 2*. Work in this book can also be used for homework but its main focus is on extension of the foundations introduced in the new syllabus.

Content and suggested activities are an extension of the syllabus guidelines and topics introduced and addressed in *New Syllabus Maths, Stage One Book 2*. Topic headings treat and develop content under these guidelines which include Number and Algebra, Measurement and Space as well as Statistics and Data.

Some additional topics have been added as Optional Extension to the Syllabus. These include Money, Angles, Lines, and Open Shapes.

While the teacher can select topics and content from any page in this book, it is suggested mental and extension activity topics follow on from topic content addressed in *New Syllabus Maths, Stage One Book 2*.

New Syllabus and Extension, Stage One Book 2 supports *New Syllabus Maths, Stage One* books with additional activities, a variety of extensions and further exposure to concept and knowledge needed to be successful in Maths.

A full set of answers is provided at the back of the book to assist students, teachers and parents.

Message to Parents

School introduces the child to knowledge, skills and learning experiences needed to be successful in the classroom and at school. However, it is the parents who nurture a child from birth establishing values, attitudes and encouragement for the child to be a good family member and a good citizen.

It is when the teacher and parent work together to reinforce the proficiencies, experience and knowledge learned at school, with the attitudes and values of the home, that a child will achieve outstanding results. The encouragement of parents and teachers together set a positive tone for the child's learning environment and progress.

As a parent you help your child learn every day. This book can assist with the learning processes needed for development of mathematics.

Enjoy the journey!

Place Value to 100

1. Write the numbers shown on the abacus and place value cards.

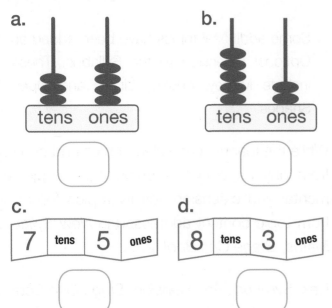

a.

tens   ones

⬜

b.

tens   ones

⬜

c.

7 **tens** 5 **ones**

⬜

d.

8 **tens** 3 **ones**

⬜

2. Write the number represented by these blocks.

a. ⬜

b. ⬜

c. ⬜

3. Add the blocks then write the totals.

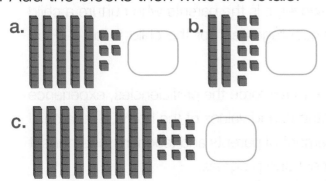

a. ⬜

b. ⬜

c. ⬜

4. Write these as numbers.

a. forty-seven ⬜   **b.** sixty-one ⬜

c. thirty-two ⬜   **d.** fifty-six ⬜

Numbers to 100

5. Match the numbers to those in words.

37	eight-three
52	seventeen
83	thirty-seven
49	fifty-two
17	forty-nine

6. Write the number **before** and **after** these.

a. _____ 29 _____   b. _____ 50 _____

c. _____ 64 _____   d. _____ 70 _____

e. _____ 35 _____   f. _____ 98 _____

7. Add these groups of ten and write their totals.

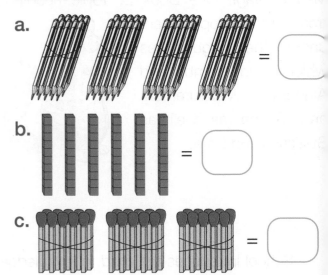

a.   = ⬜

b.   = ⬜

c.   = ⬜

8. Count how many and write the total.

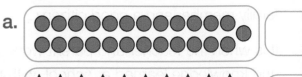

a. ⬜

b. ⬜

9. Sequence this group of numbers from 0.

12   52   74   9   18   33

0					

New Syllabus Mentals and Extension 2, Stage On

1. Write these as numbers with numerals.

a. ninety-six ☐   b. fifty-seven ☐

c. sixty-one ☐   d. twenty-five ☐

e. thirty-five ☐   f. forty-three ☐

2. Fill in the place value cards.

a. 83

tens		ones

b. 72

tens		ones

c. 25

tens		ones

d. 49

tens		ones

3. Continue each number pattern.

a. 87 88 89 ◯ ◯ ◯

b. 75 70 65 ☐ ☐ ☐

c. 30 40 50 ⬠ ⬠ ⬠

d. 27 24 21 ⬡ ⬡ ⬡

e. 24 26 28 ◯ ◯ ◯

4. Compare numbers, colour the card.

a. 43 — is larger than / is smaller than — 34

b. 86 — is larger than / is smaller than — 68

5. Counting by twos, continue the pattern.

a.
6	8			14	

b.
38	40			46	

c.
90	88			82	

6. Counting by fives, fill in the numbers to match the dots.

☐ ☐ ☐ ☐ ☐

7. Fill in this pattern counting by fives.

0									

8. Write the numbers **five more** than these.

a. 15 ☐   b. 35 ☐

c. 40 ☐   d. 67 ☐

9. Write the numbers **five less** than these.

a. ☐ 50   b. ☐ 75

c. ☐ 80   d. ☐ 38

10. Find the rule to colour the path in the pattern. Write the rule.

a.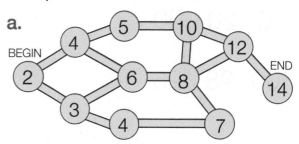

Rule: _____

b.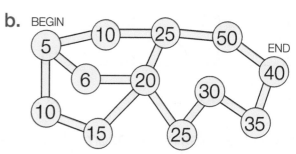

Rule: _____

11. Count the five cent coins, write the total.

     = ☐

Two-Digit Numbers to 100

1. Fill in the numbers represented by the blocks of ten.

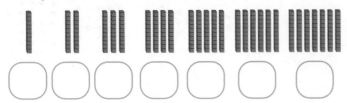

○ ○ ○ ○ ○ ○ ○

2. Complete each place value card.

a.
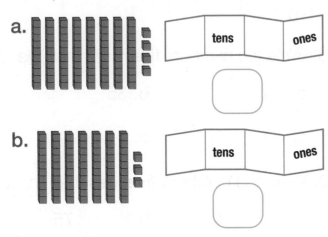

tens	ones

○

b.

tens	ones

○

3. Fill in these missing numbers.

a. 12 14 ⬠ ⬠ ⬠ ⬠

b. | 10 | 20 | 30 | | | |

c. 100 98 96 ○ ○ ○

4. Write the numbers **ten before** and **ten after** each of these numbers.

a. _____ 60 _____   b. _____ 20 _____

c. _____ 90 _____   d. _____ 10 _____

e. _____ 50 _____   f. _____ 75 _____

5. Write the missing or incorrect number in each group.

a. 🐛 0 10 30 40 50 60   ○

b. 🐛 60 50 40 20 10 0   ○

Skip Counting by Threes

6. Complete this 'skip count' pattern.

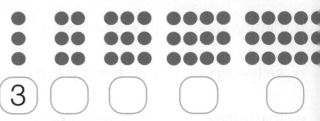

3 ○ ○ ○ ○

7. Counting by threes, complete the pattern

9	12			21	

8. Write the **3 more** and **3 less** than each of these.

a. ○ 9 ○   b. ○ 18 ○

c. ○ 21 ○   d. ○ 12 ○

9. Skip count to continue numbers in each pattern.

a. | 2 | 4 | 6 | 8 | | | |

b. | 3 | 6 | 9 | 12 | | | |

c. | 5 | 10 | 15 | 20 | | | |

d. | 10 | 20 | 30 | 40 | | | |

10. Use skip counting to add the value of each set of coins.

a.  = ○

b.  = ○

c.  =$ ○

11. Skip count to continue numbers in each pattern.

| 3 | 6 | 9 | | | |

Two-Digit Numbers to 100

1. Fill in the missing numbers in each pattern.

a.
- 8
- ( )
- ( )
- 14
- ( )
- 18

b.
- 9
- ( )
- ( )
- 18
- ( )
- 24

c.
- 5
- ( )
- ( )
- 20
- ( )
- 30

2. Add numbers across the top to those down the side to complete the table.

+	8	12	23	35	19
a. 4					
b. 7					
c. 8					
d. 6					

3. Add the missing numbers in the addition squares.

a.
8		15
5	3	
	10	23

b.
5		13
6	4	
	12	23

4. Write the next two numbers.

a. 32 _____, _____   b. 98 _____, _____

Skip Counting by Threes

5. Continue the patterns by adding the missing numbers.

a.
- 8
- 10
- 12
- ( )
- ( )
- ( )

b.
- 12
- 15
- 18
- ( )
- ( )
- ( )

c.
- 40
- 50
- 60
- ( )
- ( )
- ( )

d.
- 15
- 20
- 25
- ( )
- ( )
- ( )

6. Fill in the missing number facts.

a.
$1 \times 3 =$
$2 \times 3 =$
$3 \times 3 =$
$4 \times 3 =$
$5 \times 3 =$
$6 \times 3 =$
$7 \times 3 =$
$8 \times 3 =$
$9 \times 3 =$
$10 \times 3 =$

b.
$1 \times 2 =$
$2 \times 2 =$
$3 \times 2 =$
$4 \times 2 =$
$5 \times 2 =$
$6 \times 2 =$
$7 \times 2 =$
$8 \times 2 =$
$9 \times 2 =$
$10 \times 2 =$

7. a. Count by 5s, along the number line.

0   5   10   15   20   15   30   35   40

b. How many skips along the line to 40?

1. Colour the numbers, counting by fives.

1	2	3	4	5	6	7	8	9	10
11	12	13	14	15	16	17	18	19	20
21	22	23	24	25	26	27	28	29	30
31	32	33	34	35	36	37	38	39	40
41	42	43	44	45	46	47	48	49	50

2. Counting by fives, complete the pattern.

5	10						

3. Write the number **5 more** and **5 less** than each of these.

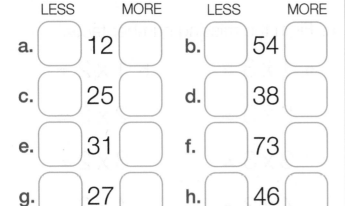

	LESS		MORE			LESS		MORE
a.		12			b.		54	
c.		25			d.		38	
e.		31			f.		73	
g.		27			h.		46	

4. Complete the patterns counting by tens.

a.
20	30	40				

b.
88	78	68				

c.
35	45	55				

5. Write numbers **ten more** and **ten less** than these.

a. ☐ 64 ☐   b. ☐ 27 ☐

c. ☐ 52 ☐   d. ☐ 38 ☐

e. ☐ 41 ☐   f. ☐ 83 ☐

6. Colour the numbers, counting by fives

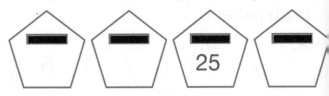

25

7. Fill in the missing numbers.

a. ⑪ ⑬ ◯ ◯ ⑲ ◯

b. | 31 | 33 | 35 | | | |

c. ⑤⑤ ⑤③ ⑤① ⬠ ⬠ ⬠

8. Complete the patterns of five.

a.
0	5		15	20	25		

b.
35	30	25					0

c.
90	85	80	75			60	

d.
47	42	37					

9. Number these letter boxes.

44

10. Count by **threes** to continue these patterns.

a.
72	75	78			

b.
65	68	71			

c.
9	12	15			

d.
36	39	42			

New Syllabus Mentals and Extension 2, Stage On

More Place Value

1. Write the number represented by these abacus and cards.

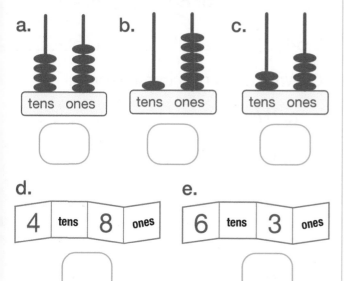

a. tens ones ( )

b. tens ones ( )

c. tens ones ( )

d. | 4 | tens | 8 | ones | ( )

e. | 6 | tens | 3 | ones | ( )

2. Fill in the place value cards.

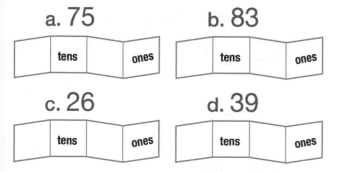

a. 75 | tens | ones |

b. 83 | tens | ones |

c. 26 | tens | ones |

d. 39 | tens | ones |

3. Add the blocks then write the totals.

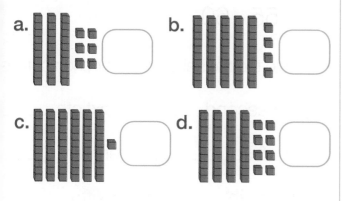

a. ( )   b. ( )

c. ( )   d. ( )

4. Write each two-digit number shown in the place value frame.

a. 76   b. 43   c. 69   d. 85

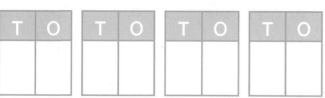

T	O	T	O	T	O	T	O

Odds and Evens

5. Colour the circles that have **odd** numbers in them.

51 62 37 57 39 24

58 66 33 25 19

6. Fill in the missing numbers on the chart.

7	8		10	
12	13	14		16
	18	19	20	
22		24		26

7. What did you notice about all the added numbers?

They are all _____ numbers.

8. Write **half** of each numbers.
   Colour the halves that have **even** halves.

a. $\frac{1}{2}$ of 12 ( )   b. $\frac{1}{2}$ of 14 ( )

c. $\frac{1}{2}$ of 36 ( )   d. $\frac{1}{2}$ of 50 ( )

e. $\frac{1}{2}$ of 62 ( )   f. $\frac{1}{2}$ of 30 ( )

9. Add each group of numbers.
   Colour the even numbered totals.

a. 6 + 7= ( )   b. 9 + 3= ( )

c. 8 + 5= ( )   d. 12 + 23= ( )

e. 18 + 7= ( )   f. 15 + 15= ( )

g. 9 + 17= ( )   h. 15 + 2= ( )

Ordinal Numbers

1. Write the order for each item.

1st   **4th**

2. Write the ordinal number that comes after each one.

a. 27th _____   b. 64th _____

c. 31st _____   d. 19th _____

e. 99th _____   f. 50th _____

g. 43rd _____   h. 22nd _____

3. Write the ordinal number that comes before each one.

a. _____ 20th   b. _____ 34th

c. _____ 43rd   d. _____ 22nd

e. _____ 50th   f. _____ 65th

4. What is the **3rd** letter of the alphabet?

5. What place comes after **7th**? _____

6. What is the **5th** day of the school week? _____

7. What is the **8th** month of the year? _____

8. What date is Christmas Day?

_____

Mixed Bag

9. Write the place value for each bold numb

a. 37 _____   b. 84 _____   c. 42 _____

d. 64 _____   e. 95 _____   f. 36 _____

10. Write each number in words.

a. 87 _____

b. 64 _____

c. 39 _____

d. 51 _____

e. 60 _____

f. 48 _____

11. Fill in the **next four** numbers.

a. 46 47 ◯ ◯ ◯ ◯

b. 68 67 ☐ ☐ ☐ ☐

c. 27 32 ⬠ ⬠ ⬠ ⬠

d. 55 60 ⬡ ⬡ ⬡ ⬡

12. Write the ordinal number for each of thes

a. sixty-second _____   b. sixtieth _____

c. forty-first _____   d. twentieth _____

e. forty-sixth _____   f. fifty-fifth _____

13. Write the even number **before** and **after** these.

a. _____ 60 _____   b. _____ 22 _____

c. _____ 57 _____   d. _____ 48 _____

e. _____ 73 _____   f. _____ 98 _____

New Syllabus Mentals and Extension 2, Stage O

1. Write this number using numerals.

87 _____

2. How many tens in 70? ⬜

3. Identify the missing number in this pattern.

| 37 | 40 | 43 | 49 | 52 | 55 | ⬜ |

4. Find the counting rule for this number path.

Rule ⬜

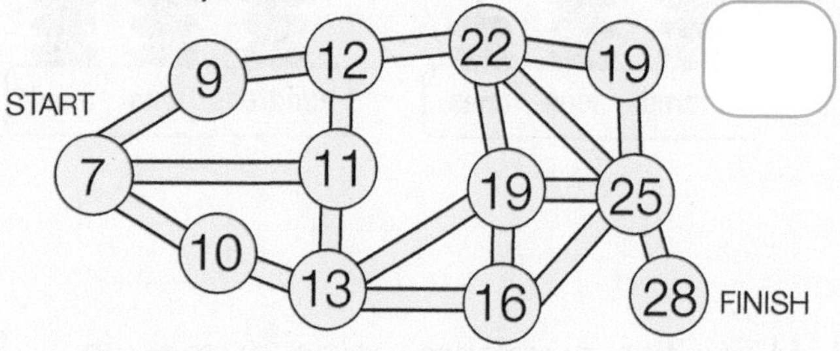

START 9 — 12 — 22 — 19
7 — 11 — 19 — 25
10 — 13 — 16 — 28 FINISH

5. Write the number shown by each group of ten.

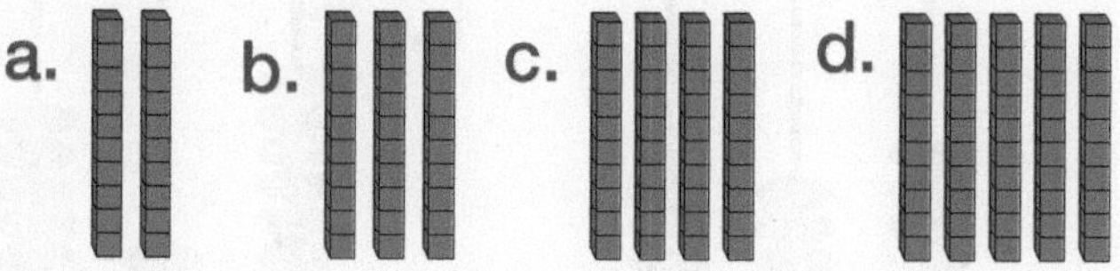

a. ⬜   b. ⬜   c. ⬜   d. ⬜

6. Add the blocks and write the number they represent. ⬜

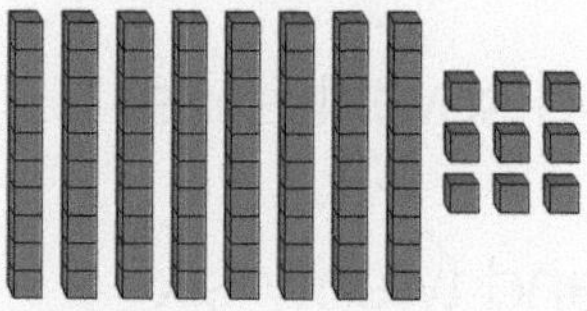

7. Write the numbers **ten more** and **ten less** than this number.

⬜ 65 ⬜

8. Compare numbers and colour the correct card.

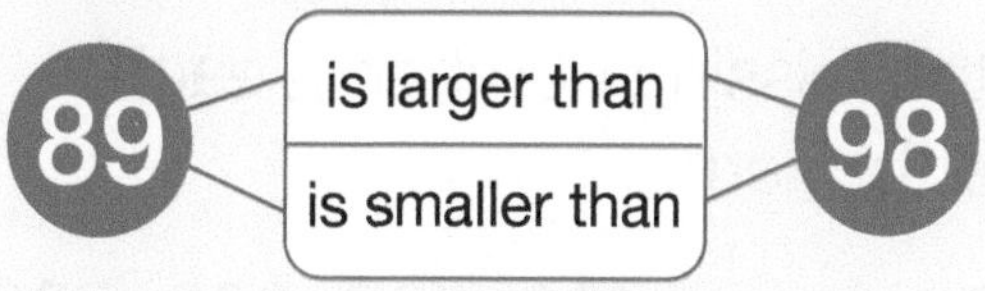

89 — is larger than / is smaller than — 98

9. How many fives in 45? ⬜

10. How many in this group? ⬜

11. Write these numbers using numerals.

a. seventy-eight ⬜

b. eighty-one ⬜

12. How much is shown with these five cent coins? ⬜

13. What is the new price for each item if reduced by $5.

a. $53   NEW PRICE

b. $68   NEW PRICE

15. Identify each of these.

a. 9th letter of the alphabet? ⬜

b. fourteenth letter? ⬜

c. 11th word of the National anthem? ⬜

14. Write the next five numbers in this pattern.

| 38 | 43 | 48 | | | | |

Place Value with Three-Digit Numbers

1. Write the numbers shown on the abacus and place value cards.

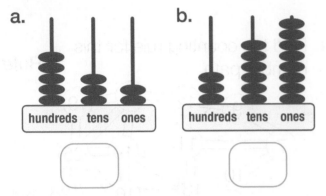

a.

b.

2. Write the numbers using numerals.

a. Six hundred and forty-four ☐

b. Five hundred and seventy-one ☐

c. Three hundred and twenty-six ☐

d. Two hundred and forty-five ☐

3. Write the missing number in each number pattern.

a. 200, _____, 400, 500, 600, 700

b. 185, _____, 195, 200, 205, 210

c. 87, 89, _____, 93, 95, 97

d. 409, 429, _____, 469, 489

4. Show these numbers on a abacus.

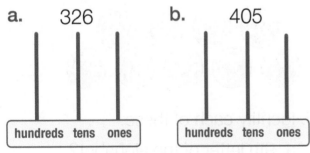

a.   326

b.   405

5. Write the numbers in counting order.

667   632   678   647   694

Numbers to 1000

6. Write these numbers on the place value cards.

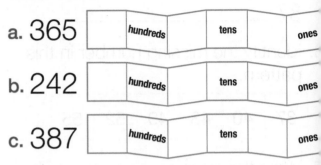

a. 365 | hundreds | tens | ones |

b. 242 | hundreds | tens | ones |

c. 387 | hundreds | tens | ones |

7. What number is shown on each abacu

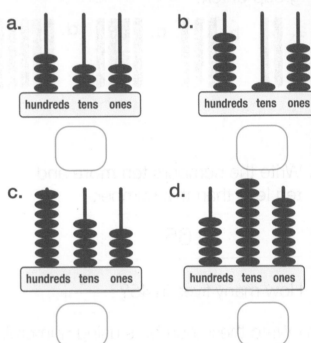

a.

b.

c.

d.

8. Write each of these as numbers.

a. six hundred and seventy-two_____

b. eight hundred and fifty-nine _____

c. two hundred and twenty _____

9. Write the whole number shown on each place value card.

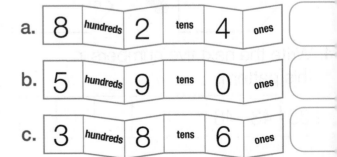

a. | 8 hundreds | 2 tens | 4 ones |

b. | 5 hundreds | 9 tens | 0 ones |

c. | 3 hundreds | 8 tens | 6 ones |

Place Value with Three-Digit Numbers

1. Show each number on an abacus.

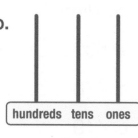

a. | b.

hundreds tens ones   hundreds tens ones

365   241

2. What numbers are shown here?

a. 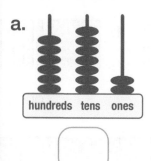   b.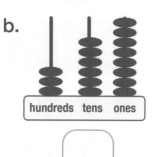

hundreds tens ones   hundreds tens ones

3. Write each number in words.

a. 453 _____

b. 228 _____

c. 167 _____

d. 479 _____

e. 573 _____

4. Write the number represented in each group.

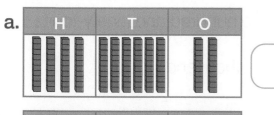

a. | H | T | O |

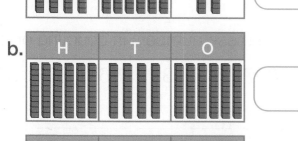

b. | H | T | O |

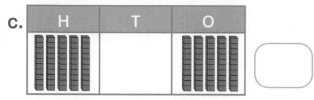

c. | H | T | O |

Three-Digit Numbers to 1000

5. Write these numbers.

a. six hundred and thirty-five _____

b. four hundred and forty-two _____

c. six hundred and one _____

d. eight hundred and sixty-two _____

e. one hundred and eighty-five _____

6. Show each number on the place value card.

a. 635

H	T	O

b. 487

H	T	O

c. 192

H	T	O

d. 706

H	T	O

7. Write these numbers.

a. $500 + 20 + 5 =$ ☐

b. $800 + 50 + 9 =$ ☐

c. $300 + 60 + 7 =$ ☐

d. $400 + 20 + 8 =$ ☐

8. Rearrange each number to a larger number.

a. 537 ☐   b. 219 ☐

c. 406 ☐   d. 283 ☐

9. Write this number in words.

1000 _____

Place Value with Hundreds Blocks

1. Write hundreds, tens and ones for these blocks.

a.
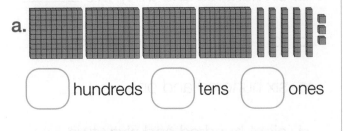

( ) hundreds ( ) tens ( ) ones

b.
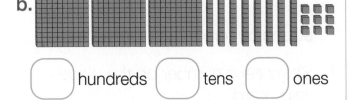

( ) hundreds ( ) tens ( ) ones

c.
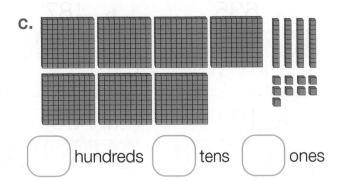

( ) hundreds ( ) tens ( ) ones

2. What number is on each place value card?

a. | 4 | hundreds | 6 | tens | 4 | ones | ( )

b. | 3 | hundreds | 9 | tens | 7 | ones | ( )

c. | 8 | hundreds | 1 | tens | 4 | ones | ( )

3. Write the number shown on each abacus.

a.
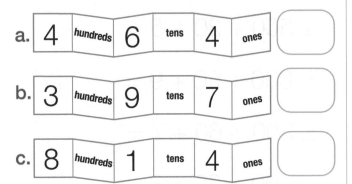
hundreds tens ones

( )

b.
hundreds tens ones

( )

Three-Digit Numbers to 1000

4. Round off each number to the nearest hundred.

a. 532 _____   b. 769 _____

c. 478 _____   d. 394 _____

e. 449 _____   f. 232 _____

5. How many ones in each group of blocks?

a.
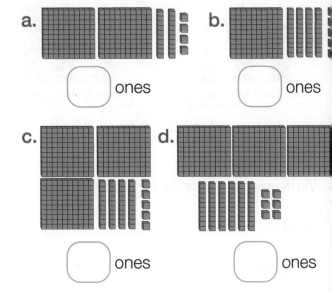
( ) ones

b.
( ) ones

c.
( ) ones

d.
( ) ones

6. Write each number.

a. six hundred and forty-six _____

b. three hundred and sixteen _____

c. eight hundred and nine _____

d. nine hundred and ninety-four _____

e. one thousand _____

7. Write these numbers in counting orde

a. 837, 649, 381, 567, 838, 94

_____ _____ _____ _____ _____

b. 519, 387, 249, 386, 549, 41

_____ _____ _____ _____ _____

Place Value and Partitioning

1. Write the number represented in each frame.

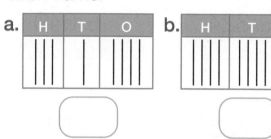

a.
H	T	O

( )

b.
H	T	O

( )

c.
H	T	O

( )

d.
H	T	O

( )

2. How many tens in each group?

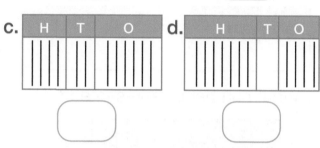

a. = ( ) b. = ( )

c. = ( ) d. = ( )

3. Partition each number into ones, tens and hundreds.

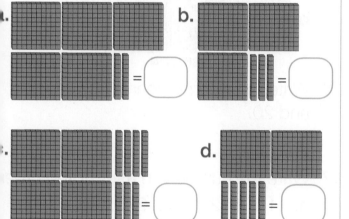

hundreds	tens	ones

a. 474 ( ) + ( ) + ( )

b. 387 ( ) + ( ) + ( )

c. 212 ( ) + ( ) + ( )

d. 708 ( ) + ( ) + ( )

4. Write the numbers shown here.

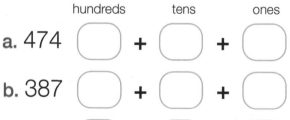

a. = ( ) b. = ( )

Place Value Three-Digit Numbers

5. Write the place value, hundred, tens or ones for each circled number.

a. 6**3**4 _____ b. 7**2**8 _____

c. 5**1**6 _____ d. 3**2**5 _____

e. 6**3**7 _____ f. 1**0**9 _____

6. Write these expanded form numbers as totals.

a. 600 + 70 + 3 = ( )

b. 700 + 30 + 2 = ( )

c. 300 + 10 + 4 = ( )

d. 100 + 7 = ( )

7. What number is shown on the place card value frames?

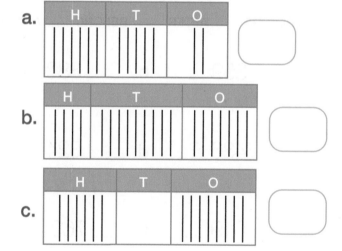

a.
H	T	O

( )

b.
H	T	O

( )

c.
H	T	O

( )

8. Write these numbers on the place value cards.

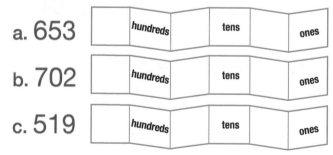

a. 653

b. 702

c. 519

9. How many tens in each of these numbers.

a. 720 ( ) b. 580 ( )

Patterns with Three-Digit Numbers	More About Numbers

1. Write the missing numbers.

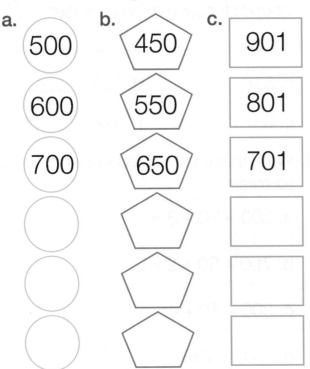

a. 500, 600, 700, ...
b. 450, 550, 650, ...
c. 901, 801, 701, ...

2. Write the number 100 **before** and **after** each of these.

BEFORE   AFTER   BEFORE   AFTER

a. ____ 359 ____   b. ____ 380 ____

c. ____ 486 ____   d. ____ 824 ____

e. ____ 619 ____   f. ____ 769 ____

g. ____ 621 ____   h. ____ 784 ____

3. Mark each number on the number line.

827   834   808   816

800   810   820   830   840

4. Show each number on a place value card.

a. 324

H	T	O

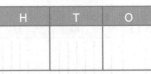

b. 649

H	T	O

c. 765

H	T	O

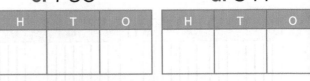

d. 317

H	T	O

5. What number is represented?

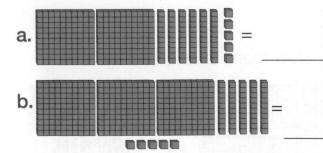

a. _____ = _____

b. _____ = _____

6. Write the **odd** numbers between 10 and 20.

____ ____ ____ ____ ____

7. Write the numbers in **ascending** order
a. 413, 872, 658, 219, 362, 390

____ ____ ____ ____ ____ ____

b. 728, 519, 372, 866, 731, 403

____ ____ ____ ____ ____ ____

8. Write four hundred and ninety-seven as a number

9. Write the **next two** numbers.

a. 799 ____,____   b. 600 ____,____

c. 249 ____,____   d. 398 ____,____

10. Write each number in words.

a. 444 _____

b. 783 _____

New Syllabus Mentals and Extension 2, Stage O

1. Colour the correct card for each path.

a.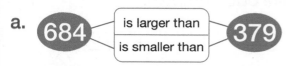

b.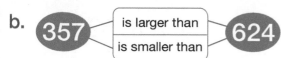

2. Fill in the missing numbers in each number sequence.

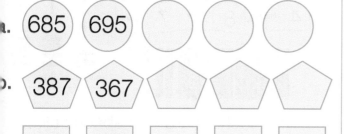

3. Write the **next two** numbers.

a. 598 ____,____ b. 701 ____,____

c. 429 ____,____ d. 299 ____,____

4. Write the numbers represented by the blocks.

a.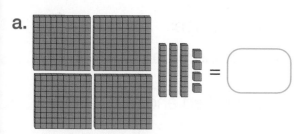

b.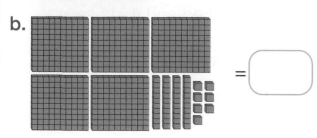

5. Write the number shown here.

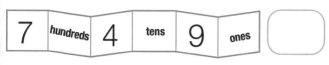

6. Round these numbers off to the nearest 100.

a. 675→_____ b. 724→_____

c. 389→_____ d. 607→_____

e. 449→_____ f. 555→_____

7. Round these numbers off to the nearest ten.

a. 143→_____ b. 317→_____

c. 574→_____ d. 212→_____

e. 178→_____ f. 516→_____

8. Read these cards then write the number to the nearest ten.

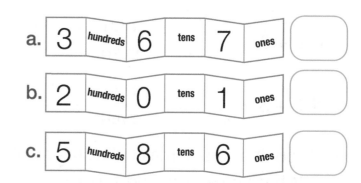

9. Write the whole number for each partitioned number.

a. 700 + 50 + 9 =

b. 500 + 30 + 2 =

c. 300 + 90 + 7 =

d. 800 + 60 + 7 =

10. Write each number.

a. six hundred and forty-six _____

b. three hundred and sixteen _____

c. eight hundred and nine _____

17

Patterns with Three-Digit Numbers

1. Colour the odd or even card for each number.

a. **647** ODD / EVEN   b. **724** ODD / EVEN

c. **571** ODD / EVEN   d. **688** ODD / EVEN

e. **600** ODD / EVEN   f. **399** ODD / EVEN

2. Add each set of numbers then colour the odd or even card's result.

a. $7 + 5 =$ ⬚ — ODD / EVEN

b. $6 + 8 =$ ⬚ — ODD / EVEN

c. $6 + 9 =$ ⬚ — ODD / EVEN

d. $8 + 3 =$ ⬚ — ODD / EVEN

3. Colour the card to match the statement.

a. When you add an odd and even number the answer is...

| always | never | sometimes | odd

b. When you add two even numbers the answer is ...

| always | never | sometimes | odd

c. When you add two odd numbers the answer is ...

| always | never | sometimes | odd

4. Halve these numbers. Colour the **even** results.

a. $\frac{1}{2}$ of $20 =$ ⬚   b. $\frac{1}{2}$ of $70 =$ ⬚

More About Numbers

5. Rearrange these numerals to make **odd** numbers.

a. 638 ⬚   b. 724 ⬚

c. 816 ⬚   d. 522 ⬚

6. What do these numbers have in common? Complete the statement.

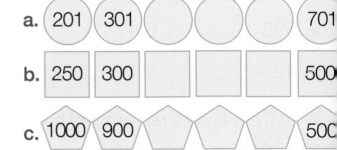

The blocks, card and abacus all.......

_____

7. Fill in the missing numbers.

a. 201 301 ◯ ◯ ◯ 701

b. 250 300 ⬚ ⬚ ⬚ 500

c. 1000 900 ⬠ ⬠ ⬠ 500

8. Write the number.

a. seven hundred and sixty-five _____

b. four hundred and forty-eight _____

c. one hundred and thirty-seven _____

d. nine hundred and ninety-two _____

9. Use the symbols > greater than or < less than to make number comparisons true.

a. 316 ⬚ 485   b. 951 ⬚ 675

c. 719 ⬚ 720   d. 864 ⬚ 51

New Syllabus Mentals and Extension 2, Stage O

. Write the number shown on these blocks.

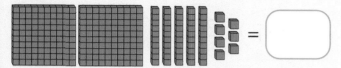 = ◯

2. Write the number.

   a. six hundred and ninety-five _____

   b. eighth hundred and fifty-six _____

   c. one hundred and nine _____

3. Show this number on the place value.

653

4. Write the numbers shown on each place value card.

a.
H	T	O
6	4	7

◯

b.
H	T	O
8	3	8

◯

5. Write the number represented here.

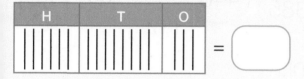 = ◯

7. Write 647 in words.
N.B. Take care with forty.

_____

_____

6. Round these numbers off to the nearest hundred.

   a. 699 _____   b. 701 _____

   c. 549 _____

9. Write the place value for the bold numbers.

   a. 4**7**3 _____   b. 68**5** _____

   c. **2**64 _____   d. 3**7**1 _____

8. Partition this number.

678 _____ + _____ + _____
     HUNDREDS   TENS   ONES

11. Arrange these numbers in **descending** order.

   416, 532, 219, 873, 458, 664

_____

10. Complete the missing numbers in each sequence.

a.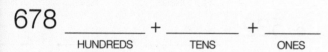

b.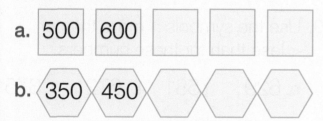

12. Write these numbers **200 more** and **200 less** than these.

   a. _____617 _____

   b. _____438 _____

13. Colour the correct card for these.

a.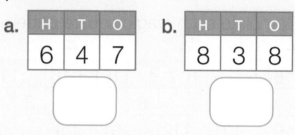

14. Rearrange these numbers to make **even** numbers.

   a. 347 _____   b. 529 _____

b.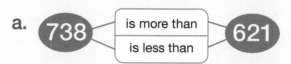

15. a. $\frac{1}{2}$ of 30 = ◯   b. $\frac{1}{2}$ of 80 = ◯

Number Patterns

1. Complete each number pattern.

a. 95 | 90 | | | |

b. 33 | 36 | | | |

c. 41 | 46 | | | |

2. Complete each magic square pattern.

a.

+	16	5	
		7	
	19		31

b.

+	7		18
		8	
	12		31

c.

−	16		11
		3	
	9		7

3. Double or halve these numbers.

a. 9 doubled ◯   **b.** 26 doubled ◯

c. 44 halved ◯   **d.** 72 halved ◯

4. Add the missing shapes to this pattern.

5. Fill in the **missing** or **incorrect** numbers in each pattern.

a. 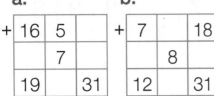 120 140 180 200 220 240 ◯

b. 98 93 88 78 73 68 ◯

6. Write numbers 100 **before** and **after** these.

a. _____ 724 _____   **b.** _____ 365 _____

More About Three-Digit Numbers

7. Colour the rounded hundreds and write them in order from **smallest to highest**.

537 300 624 500

600 593 700 865

264 200 762 131

385 448 400 251

114

ORDER

_____ _____ _____ _____ _____ ___

8. Partition this number.

a. 679 = _____ + _____ + _____
HUNDREDS   TENS   ONES

b. 418 = _____ + _____ + _____
HUNDREDS   TENS   ONES

c. 532 = _____ + _____ + _____
HUNDREDS   TENS   ONES

d. 715 = _____ + _____ + _____
HUNDREDS   TENS   ONES

9. Use the symbols > **more** than or < **less** than for these numbers.

a. 629 ◻ 581   b. 672 ◻ 375

c. 813 ◻ 954   d. 826 ◻ 715

10. Write the numbers represented here.

a. = ◯

b. = ◯

Addition Facts About Five and Ten

Fill in the missing numbers about number facts for five.

. a. $5 + 0 = 5$

b. $4 + 1 = \bigcirc$

c. $3 + 2 = \bigcirc$

d. $2 + \bigcirc = 5$

e. $1 + \bigcirc = 5$

f. $0 + 5 = \bigcirc$

2. a. $5 - 0 = \bigcirc$

b. $5 - 4 = \bigcirc$

c. $5 - \bigcirc = 2$

d. $5 - \bigcirc = 3$

e. $5 - 1 = \bigcirc$

f. $5 - \bigcirc = 5$

. Look for combinations of 10 to help add these. One is done for you.

$$\overset{\frown 10}{8+7+2} = 10+7 = 17$$

a. $6+5+4= \bigcirc$

b. $8+7+3= \bigcirc$

c. $5+4+5= \bigcirc$

d. $1+6+9= \bigcirc$

e. $3+2+8= \bigcirc$

f. $5+4+6= \bigcirc$

. Use combinations to add larger numbers.

a. $24 + 16 + 7 = \bigcirc$

b. $27 + 8 + 23 = \bigcirc$

c. $35 + 11 + 35 = \bigcirc$

. Add numbers in the top row to those down the side.

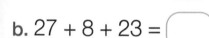

+	6	3	2	1
a. 4				
b. 7				
c. 8				
d. 9				

Addition Sentences – Algebra

6. Fill in the missing number.

a. $5 + 8 = \bigcirc \frown 13 - 5 = \bigcirc$

b. $6 + \bigcirc = 7 \frown 7 - 1 = \bigcirc$

c. $4 + \bigcirc = 10 \frown 10 - 6 = \bigcirc$

d. $7 + 3 = \bigcirc \frown \bigcirc - 3 = 7$

e. $2 + \bigcirc = 10 \frown 10 - 2 = \bigcirc$

7. Add these numbers. Look for combinations.

a. $25+14= \bigcirc$

b. $18+30= \bigcirc$

c. $51+27= \bigcirc$

d. $46+22= \bigcirc$

e. $23+16= \bigcirc$

f. $58+30= \bigcirc$

g. $29+41= \bigcirc$

h. $32+25= \bigcirc$

8. Complete the **addition** fan.

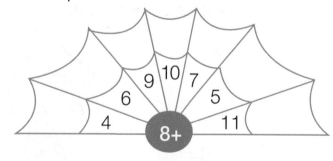

9. Complete the **subtraction** fan.

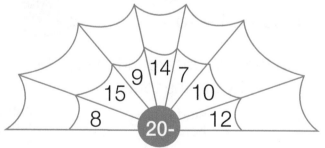

10. Add these to find totals. Look for combinations.

a. $17+13= \bigcirc$

b. $24+16= \bigcirc$

c. $38+22= \bigcirc$

d. $19+31= \bigcirc$

Addition with Concrete Material

1. Count on and complete number sentences.

a.

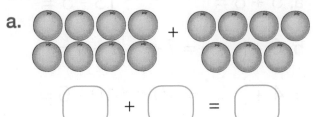

$\boxed{} + \boxed{} = \boxed{}$

b.

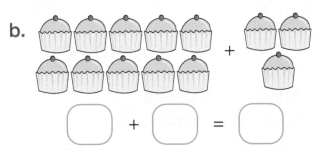

$\boxed{} + \boxed{} = \boxed{}$

c.

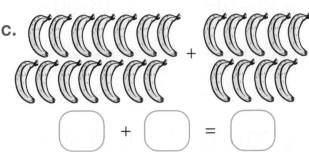

$\boxed{} + \boxed{} = \boxed{}$

2. Try these additions without concrete material. Look for combinations.

a. $13+19+7=$ $\boxed{}$

b. $34+5+16=$ $\boxed{}$

c. $27+12+8=$ $\boxed{}$

d. $35+21+15=$ $\boxed{}$

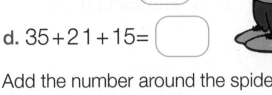

3. Add the number around the spider web and write the total.

a.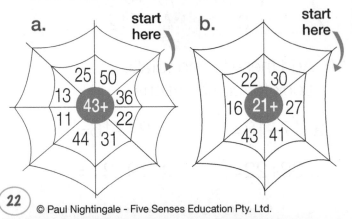

Addition on a Number Line

4. Count on to find totals. Fill in the number sentences shown on each line.

a.

$\boxed{} + \boxed{} = \boxed{}$

b.

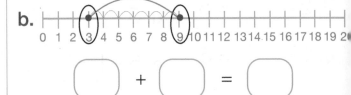

$\boxed{} + \boxed{} = \boxed{}$

c.

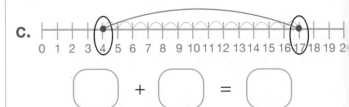

$\boxed{} + \boxed{} = \boxed{}$

5. Fill in the number sentences for these additions.

a.

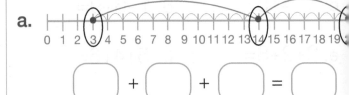

$\boxed{} + \boxed{} + \boxed{} = \boxed{}$

b.

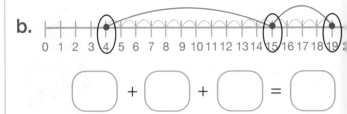

$\boxed{} + \boxed{} + \boxed{} = \boxed{}$

c.

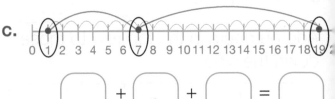

$\boxed{} + \boxed{} + \boxed{} = \boxed{}$

6. Add these numbers.

a. $6+7+4=$ $\boxed{}$ b. $8+3+6=$ $\boxed{}$

c. $5+4+9=$ $\boxed{}$ d. $2+8+9=$ $\boxed{}$

New Syllabus Mentals and Extension 2, Stage O

. Show the partitioning of the bigger number in each addition. Add the total. One is done for you.

$17+2=\bigcirc$

$(10+7+2)$

a. $17+2=\bigcirc$
$(\quad)$

b. $15+3=\bigcirc$
$(\quad)$

c. $14+3=\bigcirc$
$(\quad)$

d. $11+7=\bigcirc$
$(\quad)$

e. $13+6=\bigcirc$
$(\quad)$

. Use combinations to find totals. Add brackets first.

a. $6+(3+7)=\bigcirc$

b. $(8+2)+4=\bigcirc$

c. $9+(6+4)=\bigcirc$

d. $10+(5+5)=\bigcirc$

e. $(7+3)+4=\bigcirc$

f. $10+(3+5)=\bigcirc$

g. $(9+1)+7=\bigcirc$

h. $20+(3+6)=\bigcirc$

. Partition these additions into vertical frames.

a. $13+6 =$ | Tens | Ones |
TOTAL

b. $15+3 =$ | Tens | Ones |
TOTAL

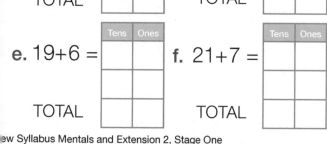

c. $14+3 =$ | Tens | Ones |
TOTAL

d. $12+6 =$ | Tens | Ones |
TOTAL

e. $19+6 =$ | Tens | Ones |
TOTAL

f. $21+7 =$ | Tens | Ones |
TOTAL

4. Write totals in each group, then tick to record the pattern rule.

a. $1+1=\bigcirc$ **b.** $2+2=\bigcirc$ **c.** $3+3=\bigcirc$

d. $4+4=\bigcirc$ **e.** $5+5=\bigcirc$ **f.** $6+6=\bigcirc$

g. $7+7=\bigcirc$ **h.** $8+8=\bigcirc$ **i.** $9+9=\bigcirc$

Rule: Doubles by 2s $\bigcirc$ 3s $\bigcirc$ 5s $\bigcirc$

5. Double these numbers then colour the correct statement path.

a. 9 _____ **b.** 12 _____ **c.** 4 _____

d. 17 _____ **e.** 25 _____ **f.** 32 _____

g. 26 _____ **h.** 41 _____ **i.** 39 _____

When doubling a number

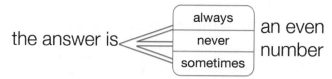

the answer is ──── always / never / sometimes ──── an even number

6. Halve these numbers then colour the correct statement path.

a. 10 _____ **b.** 20 _____ **c.** 30 _____

d. 16 _____ **e.** 8 _____ **f.** 36 _____

g. 100 _____ **h.** 18 _____ **i.** 38 _____

When halving a number

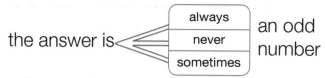

the answer is ──── always / never / sometimes ──── an odd number

7. Colour the numbers that when halved the result is an **odd** number.

| 34 | 62 | 48 | 26 |

| 80 | 52 | 98 |

Vertical Addition	Vertical Addition with Regrouping

Vertical Addition

1. Add the blocks.

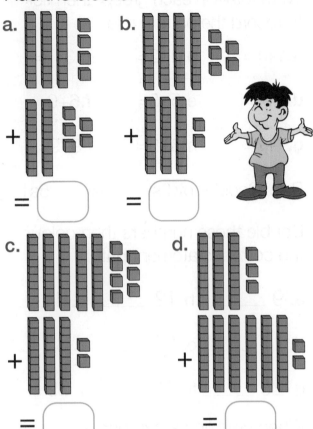

a. =

b. =

c. =

d. =

2. Add the numbers in each frame.

a.

Tens	Ones
6	2
+ 2	5

b.

Tens	Ones
4	4
+ 2	5

c.

Tens	Ones
6	2
+ 2	7

d.

Tens	Ones
3	5
+ 2	3

e.

Tens	Ones
4	1
+ 2	6

f.

Tens	Ones
3	7
+ 4	2

3. A farmer had 42 sheep in one paddock and 43 in another. How many does he have in total? Use the frame to write the algorithm.

Tens	Ones
+	

Vertical Addition with Regrouping

Regroup the ones when greater than 10 to tens and ones.

= 5

$$\begin{array}{r} 10 \\ + 5 \\ \hline 15 \end{array}$$

4. Add these blocks. Regroup the ones to 10s and ones.

a.

T	O

b.

T	O

c.

T	O

d.

T	O

5. Write the vertical addition. Regroup the ones to a ten, then add. One is done.

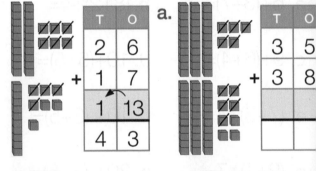

T	O
2	6
+ 1	7
1	13
4	3

a.

T	O
3	5
+ 3	8

b.

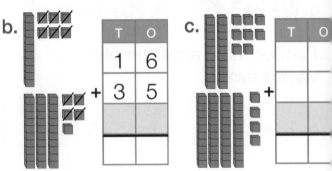

T	O
1	6
+ 3	5

c.

T	O
+	

6. Try these without the blocks. Regroup ones to a ten then add it to the 10's column.

a.

T	O
4	8
+ 2	9

b.

T	O
6	8
+ 1	8

c.

T	O
5	4
+ 3	7

1. Regroup ones to tens when the ones column is greater than 10. Complete the vertical additions. One is done for you.

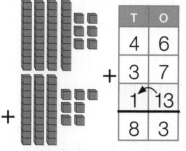

	T	O
	4	6
+	3	7
	1	⟋13
	8	3

a.

	T	O
	2	7
+	3	8

b.

	T	O
	4	6
+	1	9

c.

	T	O
	3	5
+	2	7

d.

	T	O
	3	6
+	2	8

e.

	T	O
	4	7
+	2	6

f.

	T	O
	3	8
+	5	4

2. The baker had 24 loaves of bread in one tray and 39 in another. How many in total?

	T	O
+		

3. Add the numbers in each frame.

a.

	H	T	O
	3	4	7
+	1	2	5

b.

	H	T	O
	4	2	8
+	2	3	6

c.

	H	T	O
	1	3	6
+	4	4	7

d.

	H	T	O
	2	3	5
+	3	2	8

4. Add by regrouping the ones column to a ten.

a.

	H	T	O
	1	2	7
+	6	3	4

b.

	H	T	O
	2	5	8
+	3	2	7

c.

	H	T	O
	5	1	7
+	3	2	4

d.

	H	T	O
	6	4	9
+	1	4	6

5. Add by regrouping the tens column to a hundred.

a.

	H	T	O
	3	2	5
+	6	3	4

b.

	H	T	O
	4	5	8
+	3	3	9

c.

	H	T	O
	5	4	7
+	3	2	6

d.

	H	T	O
	6	4	6
+	2	3	6

6. PROBLEM

Mohammed had saved $264, his sister Amira had saved $327. How much did they have altogether?

$⬚ + $⬚ = $⬚

1. Fill in the missing numbers for these additions.

a. 9 + 7 = ◯   b. 6 + ◯ = 11

2. Add these numbers. Look for combinations.

a. 25 + 9 + 15 = ◯

b. 31 + 19 + 3 = ◯

3. Add the missing number to these.

a. 17 + ◯ + 7 = 34

b. 8 + 15 + ◯ + 7 = 33

4. Write the missing numbers in the magic squares.

a.
+	6	7	
		9	
12		28	

b.
+	9		13
		7	
15		26	

5. Count the apples then write the number sentence with the total.

◯ + ◯ = ◯ apples

6. Add these numbers around each wagon wheel.

a.

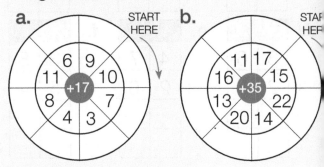

b.

7. Fill in the addition sentence shown on the number line.

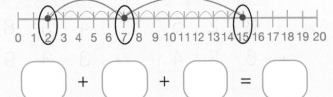

◯ + ◯ + ◯ = ◯

8. Double these numbers.

a. 9   b. 23   c. 46

◯   ◯   ◯

9. Fill in the number sentence shown on the blocks.

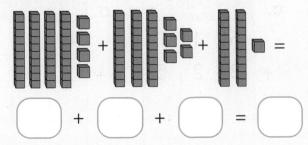

◯ + ◯ + ◯ = ◯

10. Add the numbers in each frame.

a.
H	T	O
4	4	5
3	1	8

b.
H	T	O
2	4	6
5	1	3

11. Add these with regrouping.

a.
H	T	O
2	4	7
3	1	8

b.
H	T	O
1	2	8
6	3	4

12. Nixon had 118 coloured pencils. Kobe had 234 pencils and Bowie had 121. How many pencils did the boys have altogether?

H	T	O

New Syllabus Mentals and Extension 2, Stage O

1. Count on and complete number sentences.

a.

◯ – ◯ = ◯

b.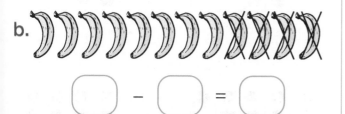

◯ – ◯ = ◯

c.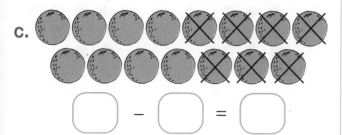

◯ – ◯ = ◯

2. Fill in the missing numbers for these.

a. $18 - 8 =$ ◯   b. $17 - 6 =$ ◯

c. ◯ $- 8 = 11$ d. $23 -$ ◯ $= 6$

e. $28 -$ ◯ $= 12$ f. $42 - 6 =$ ◯

g. ◯ $- 16 = 9$ h. ◯ $- 11 = 5$

3. Subtract each number on the outside from the centre one. Use a calculator.

START HERE

4. Fill in the number sentence for each subtraction model.

a.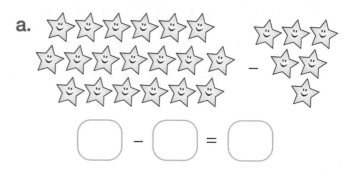

◯ – ◯ = ◯

b.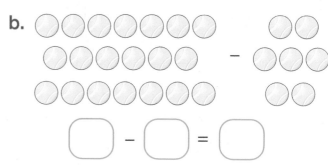

◯ – ◯ = ◯

5. Use the removal method to take away and complete the number sentence.

a. $22 - 11 =$ ◯   b. $16 - 9 =$ ◯

c. $18 - 7 =$ ◯   d. $19 - 6 =$ ◯

e. $27 - 13 =$ ◯   f. $18 - 9 =$ ◯

6. Fill in the missing number in each subtraction.

a. $19 -$ ◯ $= 7$ b. $15 -$ ◯ $= 4$

c. $24 -$ ◯ $= 10$ d. $32 - 7 =$ ◯

e. $27 -$ ◯ $= 9$ f. ◯ $- 8 = 12$

g. ◯ $- 11 = 13$ h. ◯ $- 5 = 11$

27

Subtraction

1. Count backwards along the number line to find how many taken away. Fill in the number sentence for each.

a.

◯ − ◯ = ◯

b.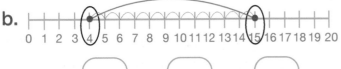

◯ − ◯ = ◯

c.

◯ − ◯ = ◯

d.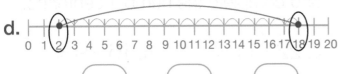

◯ − ◯ = ◯

2. Show the number sentence on each number line. Complete the sentence.

a. 18 - 9 = ◯

b. 20 - 14 = ◯

3. Take numbers down the side from numbers across the top.

—	18	27	39	46	38	26
a. 15						
b. 11						
c. 16						

Subtraction Number Sentences

4. Count each group then the crossed off. Fill in the numbers sentence to match.

a. 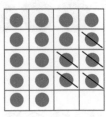   **b.**

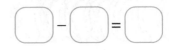
◯ − ◯ = ◯   ◯ − ◯ = ◯

c. 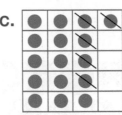   **d.**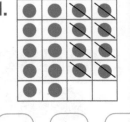

◯ − ◯ = ◯   ◯ − ◯ = ◯

5. Use the number line to count backwards and find the difference for each sentence.

a. 15 − 8 = ◯   **b.** 18 − 7 = ◯

c. 12 − 9 = ◯   **d.** 20 − 9 = ◯

e. 19 − 7 = ◯   **f.** 17 − 10 = ◯

6. PROBLEMS - Fill in the number sentences.

a. Nixon had 24 cakes. He gave 3 to Kobe and 4 to Bowie. How many did he have left?

◯ − ◯ = ◯

b. Kurt scored 19 runs in the total of 67 for the team. How many runs did the rest of the team score?

◯ − ◯ = ◯

New Syllabus Mentals and Extension 2, Stage O

. Take away the blocks at the bottom from those at the top.

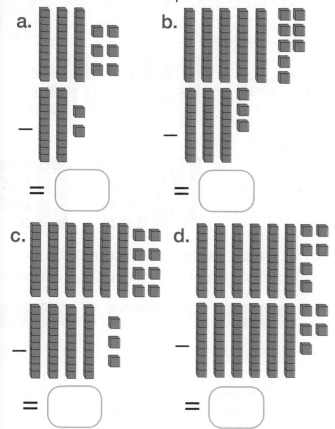

a.

= ◯

b.

= ◯

c.

= ◯

d.

= ◯

. Try subtraction using numbers.

a.
Tens	Ones
4	8
− 2	6

b.
Tens	Ones
7	8
− 4	4

c.
Tens	Ones
5	9
− 2	5

d.
Tens	Ones
4	6
− 3	3

e.
Tens	Ones
7	5
− 3	4

f.
Tens	Ones
8	7
− 5	2

. I had 64 marbles and lost 23 to my friend Jessie.

How many do I have left? Use the frame.

Tens	Ones
−	

I had ◯ left.

4. Write the vertical subtraction and totals shown on the place value cards.

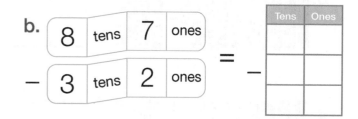

a. 7 tens 6 ones − 2 tens 3 ones =

Tens	Ones
−	

b. 8 tens 7 ones − 3 tens 2 ones =

Tens	Ones
−	

c. 6 tens 9 ones − 3 tens 4 ones =

Tens	Ones
−	

5. Write the vertical subtraction and totals with three-digit numbers.

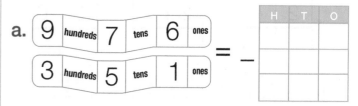

a. 9 hundreds 7 tens 6 ones − 3 hundreds 5 tens 1 ones =

H	T	O
−		

b. 8 hundreds 8 tens 4 ones − 2 hundreds 5 tens 2 ones =

H	T	O
−		

c. 8 hundreds 6 tens 5 ones − 5 hundreds 0 tens 4 ones =

H	T	O
−		

6. Complete these three-digit subtractions.

a.
H	T	O
7	8	7
− 2	1	6

b.
H	T	O
5	3	7
− 2	1	5

c.
H	T	O
6	8	7
− 2	7	2

1. Fill in the subtraction frame and write differences.

a.

Tens	Ones
−	

b.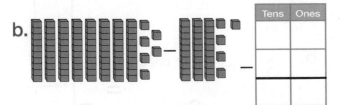

Tens	Ones
−	

c.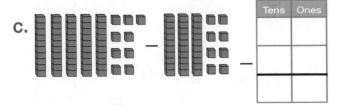

Tens	Ones
−	

2. Try these two-digit subtractions without blocks.

a.
Tens	Ones
7	6
− 2	4

b.
Tens	Ones
5	4
− 2	1

c.
Tens	Ones
7	9
− 3	6

d.
Tens	Ones
8	5
− 1	2

e.
Tens	Ones
4	9
− 1	7

f.
Tens	Ones
6	7
− 3	2

3. Complete these three-digit subtractions.

a.
H	T	O
6	8	3
− 1	2	0

b.
H	T	O
4	7	9
− 1	2	3

c.
H	T	O
8	5	4
− 2	1	3

d.
H	T	O
6	7	9
− 4	3	1

Regroup one ten block to ten ones and write it in the ones column. Cross of that one ten.

T	O
3	13
~~4~~	~~3~~
2	7
− 1	6

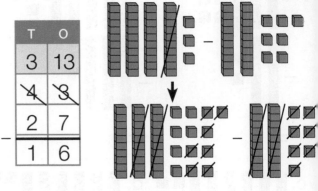

4. Regroup one ten to ten ones, then continue the subtraction. One is done.

T	O
5	13
~~6~~	~~3~~
− 2	5
3	8

a.
T	O
3	7
− 1	9

b.
T	O
6	3
− 3	7

c.
T	O
8	2
− 2	6

d.
T	O
4	6
− 2	8

e.
T	O
6	0
− 3	2

f.
T	O
4	3
− 1	7

g.
T	O
8	3
− 2	8

h.
T	O
3	3
− 1	7

5. Mum made 36 cup cakes. We ate 18 of them at lunch. How many left. (Use the frame)

T	O
−	

. Subtract the outside number from the one in the middle.

START HERE

34	26
51	63
78-	
70	35
42	67

. Regroup one ten to ones. Take off one ten and find the difference. One is done.

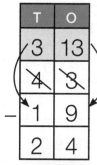

T	O
3	13
4	3
− 1	9
2	4

a.

T	O
6	5
− 1	8

b.

T	O
7	2
− 3	8

c.

T	O
2	4
− 1	7

d.

T	O
6	6
− 2	9

e.

T	O
7	1
− 3	7

f.

T	O
4	3
− 1	8

g.

T	O
8	7
− 2	8

h.

T	O
8	1
− 3	2

. Mum had $92 to do the shopping at the supermarket. The bill came to $56. How much did she have left? (Use the frame)

T	O
−	
$	

4. Regroup one tens to ones. Take off one ten and find the difference.

a.

H	T	O
6	7	4
− 3	2	7

b.

H	T	O
8	9	5
− 4	6	4

c.

H	T	O
3	7	3
− 1	4	6

d.

H	T	O
6	9	5
− 1	3	8

5. Regroup hundreds for tens. Take off one hundred and complete the frames.

a.

H	T	O
6	4	8
− 1	7	2

b.

H	T	O
9	3	7
− 3	8	4

6. Complete these subtractions. Look for combinations.

a. 44 - 31 = ⬚   b. 78 - 36= ⬚

c. 58 - 27 = ⬚   d. 63 - 40= ⬚

e. 87 - 24 = ⬚   g. 56 - 42= ⬚

f. 76 - 36= ⬚   h. 55 - 32= ⬚

7. a. Mahika is 9 years old. Her mother is 25 years older. How old is Mahika's mother?_____

b. Amed had 48 apps on his mobile phone. He deleted half of them. How many left? _____

1. Complete these operations. One is done.

a. 19 - 7 = [12] + 7 = [19]

b. 23 - 8 = [ ] + 8 = [ ]

c. 17 - 10 = [ ] + 10 = [ ]

d. 46 - 2 = [ ] + 2 = [ ]

e. 18 - 11 = [ ] + 11 = [ ]

f. 27 - 14 = [ ] + 14 = [ ]

2. Subtract the numbers around the wheel from the centre number.

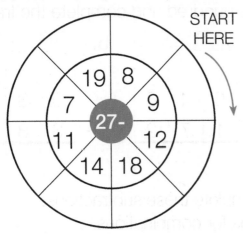

START HERE

27 -
19 8
7   9
11   12
14 18

3. Add the numbers down the side to those across the top.

+	25	32	19	12	17
a. 7					
b. 8					
c. 6					

4. Simon had 34 football cards. 16 were lost in the washing machine. How many does he have left?

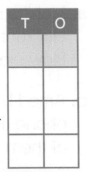

T	O
−	

5. Fill in the subtraction number sentences for these additions.

a. 27-13 = [ ]   [ ] + [ ] = 2?

b. 38 - [ ] = 23   [ ] + 23 = 38

c. 25 + 14 = [ ]   [ ] - 25 = 14

d. 32 + 17 = [ ]   [ ] - 32 = 17

6. Write the missing numbers in each magic square.

a.
+		
4	8	
	7	16
13		28

b.
-		
18	12	
	5	2
11		4

7. Take the numbers down the side from those in the top row.

−	18	27	39	46	38	26
a. 15						
b. 11						
c. 16						

MORE PROBLEMS -
Write number sentences.

8. a. Ali had collected 62 footy cards during the footy season. He gave half to his brother Mohammed. How many did he have left?

[ ] − [ ] = [ ] left

b. Alena saved $12 in June, $17 in August and $35 in October from he paper run. How much did she save

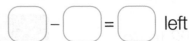

[ ] + [ ] + [ ] = $ [ ]

1. Write the number sentence for the cross off method model.

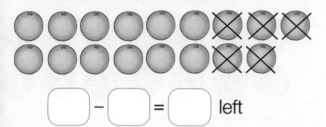

◯ - ◯ = ◯ left

2. Find the differences.

a. 35 - 21 = ◯   b. 63 - 24 = ◯

3. Fill in the number sentence to match the information on the number line.

◯ - ◯ = ◯

4. Fill in the number sentence to match the subtraction frame.

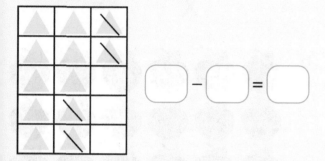

◯ - ◯ = ◯

5. Fill in the subtraction frame to match the blocks.

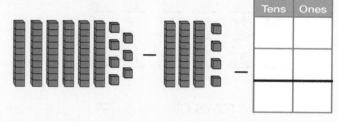

Tens	Ones

6. Fill in the vertical subtraction for the place value cards.

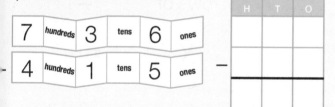

7 hundreds 3 tens 6 ones

- 4 hundreds 1 tens 5 ones

H	T	O

7. Complete these subtractions.

a.

H	T	O
7	6	4
- 3	2	3

b. 757
   - 246
   _____

8. Regroup to complete these subtractions.

a.

H	T	O
4	6	6
- 1	2	8

b.

H	T	O
8	7	4
- 3	4	9

c.

H	T	O
5	8	2
- 1	3	6

9. Fill in the missing numbers.

a. 16 - 5 = ◯   ◯ + 5 = 16

b. 37 - ◯ = 12   12 + ◯ = 37

10. Subtract numbers from the centre.

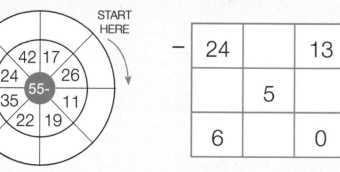

11. Complete the magic square.

-	24		13
		5	
	6		0

PROBLEM

12. Paris drove her car 26 kilometres last week. The week before she only drove half that distance. How far did she drive that week?

◯ kilometres

1. Count how many objects in each row. Write a number sentence.

a. 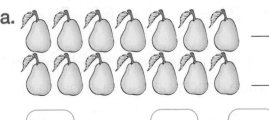 _____

 [ ] rows of [ ] = [ ]

b. 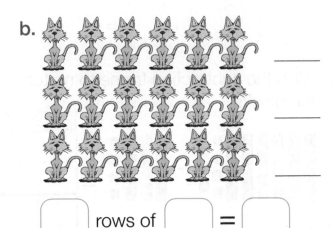 _____ _____ _____

[ ] rows of [ ] = [ ]

2. Count how many in each group.

a.

[ ] groups of [ ] = [ ]

b.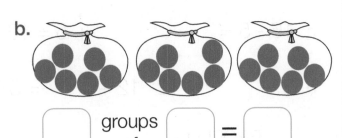

[ ] groups of [ ] = [ ]

3. Draw 10 triangles into two equal groups.

[   ] [   ]

[ ] groups of [ ] = [ ]

4. Write the multiplication sentence for each array, group or row. The multiplication sign X is used.

a.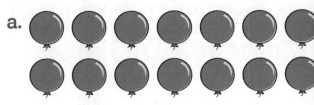

[ ] rows of [ ] = [ ]

[ ] X [ ] = [ ]

b.

[ ] rows of [ ] = [ ]

[ ] X [ ] = [ ]

5. Write the number sentence for these.

a. 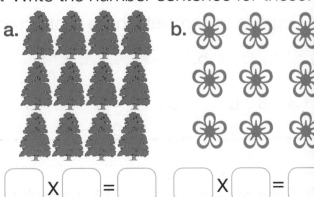 b.

[ ] X [ ] = [ ]   [ ] X [ ] = [ ]

6. Try these without pictures.

a. 8 x 2 = [ ]   b. 3 x 5 = [ ]

c. 2 x 9 = [ ]   d. 2 x 7 = [ ]

e. 5 x 5 = [ ]   f. 5 x 4 = [ ]

. The number lines show continued addition for multiplication. Fill in the number sentence as multiplication with totals.

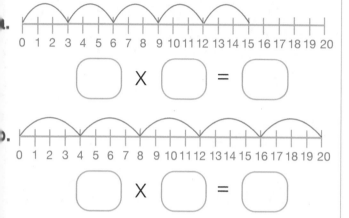

a.
◯ X ◯ = ◯

b.
◯ X ◯ = ◯

. Mark each of these on the number line.

a. 3 x 6 = ◯

b. 2 x 9 = ◯

. Count the number in each group and write the number sentence.

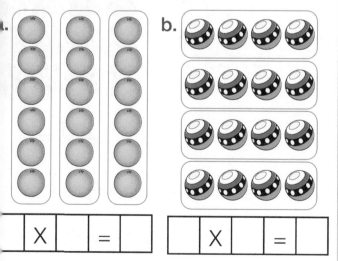

a. ☐ X ☐ = ☐   b. ☐ X ☐ = ☐

. Complete these number sentences.

a. 3 x 4 = ◯   b. 2 x 7 = ◯

c. 5 x 4 = ◯   d. 3 x 6 = ◯

5. Count the groups and rows and write the number sentences.

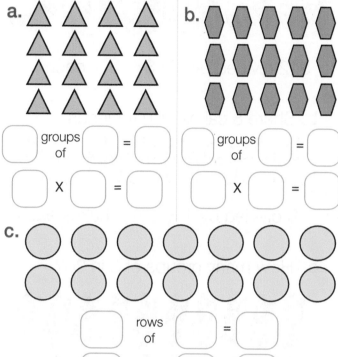

a.
◯ groups of ☐ = ◯
◯ X ◯ = ◯

b.
◯ groups of ☐ = ◯
◯ X ◯ = ◯

c.
◯ rows of ☐ = ◯
◯ X ◯ = ◯

6. Multiplication using the sign X.

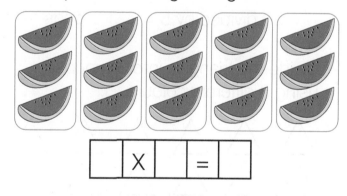

☐ X ☐ = ☐

7. Complete each number sentence.

a. 3 x 4 = ◯   b. 2 x 6 = ◯

c. 5 x 4 = ◯   d. 10 x 2 = ◯

8. PROBLEM

Hannah had $5, Eric had $5, Ishani had $5 and Ahmad had $5.

How much did the children have in total? Fill in the number sentence.

Remember the sign ◯ X ◯ = $ ◯

Division with Concrete Material

1. a. Share $12 between 3 boys.

$12 divided by 3 = $ ⬚ each

b. Share 8 cakes with 4 friends.

8 divided by 4 = ⬚ cakes each.

c. How many groups of 5 in 20?

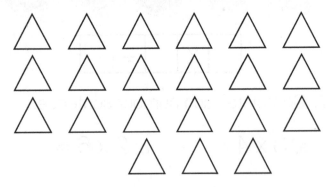

20 divided by 5 = ⬚ pegs

2. Divide the triangles into 3 groups using 3 different colours.

△ △ △ △ △ △
△ △ △ △ △ △
△ △ △ △ △ △
△ △ △

⬚ triangles divided into ⬚ = ⬚

3. a. How many groups of 6 in 12?

There are _____

b. How many groups of 5 in 30?

There are _____

Dividing Groups

4. Count the number in each group, then divide.

a. Divide by 3

⬚ ÷ 3 = ⬚

b. Divide by 2

⬚ ÷ 2 = ⬚

c. Divide by 5

⬚ ÷ 3 = ⬚

d. Divide by 10

⬚ ÷ 10 = ⬚

e. Divide by 2

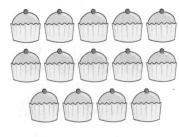

⬚ ÷ 2 = ⬚

f. Divide by 2

⬚ ÷ 2 = ⬚

5. Try these divisions without pictures.

a. $12 \div 3 =$ ⬚   **b.** $15 \div 3 =$ ⬚

c. $30 \div 3 =$ ⬚   **d.** $18 \div 3 =$ ⬚

e. $25 \div 5 =$ ⬚   **f.** $30 \div 5 =$ ⬚

Division Using a Number Line

. The number line shows continued subtraction for division. Fill in the sentences for each of these.

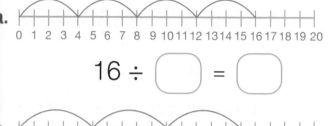

$$16 \div \boxed{} = \boxed{}$$

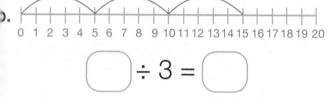

$$\boxed{} \div 3 = \boxed{}$$

. Mark each of these on the number line.

a. $14 \div 2 = \boxed{}$

b. $12 \div 4 = \boxed{}$

. Write the division sentence for each group of objects.

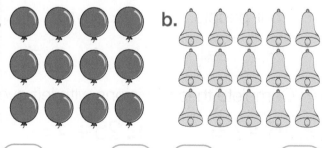

b.

$$\boxed{} \div 3 = \boxed{} \qquad \boxed{} \div 5 = \boxed{}$$

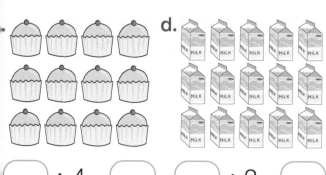

d.

$$\boxed{} \div 4 = \boxed{} \qquad \boxed{} \div 3 = \boxed{}$$

Dividing Sentences and Left Overs

4. Complete these divisions.

a. $18 \div 2 = \boxed{}$ b. $21 \div 3 = \boxed{}$

c. $30 \div 5 = \boxed{}$ d. $60 \div 10 = \boxed{}$

e. $15 \div 3 = \boxed{}$ f. $14 \div 2 = \boxed{}$

5. Count the fruit then divide them into groups. Fill in the sentence and show the left overs.

a.

$$\boxed{} \div 2 \boxed{} \text{ and } \boxed{} \text{ left over}$$

b.

$$\boxed{} \div 3 \boxed{} \text{ and } \boxed{} \text{ left over}$$

c.

$$\boxed{} \div 3 \boxed{} \text{ and } \boxed{} \text{ left over}$$

6. Complete these divisions with left overs.

a. $18 \div 2 = \boxed{}$ b. $20 \div 6 = \boxed{}$

$\boxed{}$ left over $\boxed{}$ left over

c. $25 \div 6 = \boxed{}$ d. $31 \div 10 = \boxed{}$

$\boxed{}$ left over $\boxed{}$ left over

7. Complete each problem's number sentence.

a. Share $15 equally between 3 people.

b. Share $40 equally between 10 people.

$$\boxed{} \div \boxed{} = \$ \boxed{} \qquad \boxed{} \div \boxed{} = \$ \boxed{}$$

1. How many groups of 4 in this array?

2. Write the number sentence for these groups of counters.

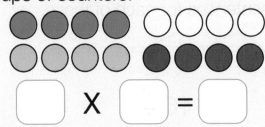

☐ X ☐ = ☐

3. Complete these sentences.

a. $5 \times 3 =$ ☐   b. $6 \times 4 =$ ☐

c. $2 \times 7 =$ ☐   d. $5 \times 6 =$ ☐

4. Write the number sentence for the row of five cent coins.

☐ X ☐ = ☐ cents

5. Fill in the number sentence shown by the number line.

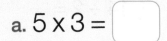

0 1 2 3 4 5 6 7 8 9 10 11 12 13 14 15 16 17 18 19 20

☐ X ☐ = ☐

6. Share $18 between 3 students.

$18 \div 3 = \$$ ☐ each

7. Divide these groups by 2 and 5.

a. 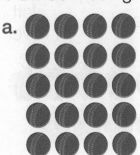   b.

☐ $\div 2 =$ ☐   ☐ $\div 5 =$ ☐

8. PROBLEMS

a. Twenty pencils shared between four people.

b. 24 footy cards shared between 2 boys.

☐ $\div$ ☐ = ☐   ☐ $\div$ ☐ = ☐

9. Fill in the division sentence shown on the number line.

0 1 2 3 4 5 6 7 8 9 10 11 12 13 14 15 16 17 18 19 20

☐ $\div 4 =$ ☐

10. Complete these divisions with left over

a. $16 \div 7 =$ ☐   b. $25 \div 4 =$ ☐

☐ left over   ☐ left over

11. Divide the side number into top number to complete the table.

÷	10	20	30	40	50	60	70
a. 2							
b. 5							
c. 10							

12. Multiply numbers down the side with those on the top line.

X	2	3	4	6	7	11
a. 2						
b. 3						
c. 5						

New Syllabus Mentals and Extension 2, Stage C

. Write the co-ordinates for each object.

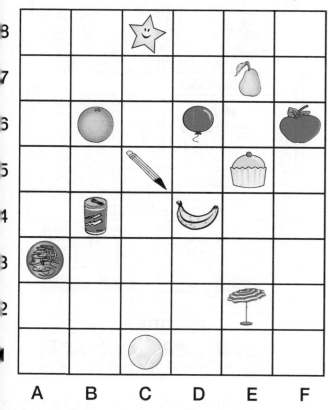

a. cupcake _____ b. banana _____

c. drink can _____ d. star _____

e. tennis
   ball _____

f. twenty
   cents _____

. What can be found at each grid
reference.

a. E7 _____ b. B6 _____

c. C5 _____ d. E5 _____

e. E2 _____ f. F6 _____

. Draw an icecream at A8

. Draw another pencil at D7

. Draw a cup at F3

. What is at D6? _____

. Draw another tennis ball at B2.

. Write your initials at F8.

ew Syllabus Mentals and Extension 2, Stage One

9.

3	6	9	12	15	18
22	24	26	28	30	32
10	20	30	40	50	60
5	15	25	35	45	55
100	95	90	85	80	75

a. What number is **above** 40? ⬭

b. Write the number **left** of 25. ⬭

c. Write the number
   two squares **below** 24. ⬭

d. Write the two numbers
   to the **right** of 28. ⬭ ⬭

e. How many numbers
   to the **left** of 80? ⬭

10. a. Line one skip
    counts by how many? _____

b. Line three skip counts by _____

c. Line four skip counts by _____

11. Write the numbers
    in the direction of
    the arrows near 40.

12. Here is a line of shapes. Write each
    shape's position on the line.

a. ✚ ___ b. E ___ c. 8 ___

d. ⬠ ___ e. O ___ f. X ___

g. Z ___ h. F ___ i. I ___

1. Starting at X, continue writing directions for the dog to find his bone.

Directions:

Forward 2 spaces _____

_____

_____

_____

2.

a. What food is
first in line? _____

b. What is the next fruit
right of the orange? _____

c. What food is **between**
orange and apple? _____

d. What item is **4th**? _____

e. What item is to the
left of the cup cake? _____

f. What two items are _____
left of the banana? _____

Finding streets and places.

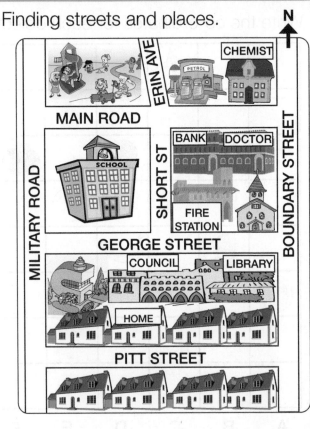

3. In which street is the Council Chambers

_____

4. The chemist is on the corner of

_____ and _____

5. What street is between George and Main

_____

6. Which street has rows of houses?

_____

7. What is on the corner of George
and Boundary Streets?

_____

8. Where is the bank? _____

_____

9. What streets meet Military Road?

_____

10. Is the doctor opposite
the chemist shop?   Yes ☐   No ☐

11. Name the streets that run East-West.

_____

New Syllabus Mentals and Extension 2, Stage

Location

. What is to the **left** of the house?

_____

. What is to the **right** of the house?

_____

. What is standing **next** to the water tank?

_____

. Draw a tree **between** the garage and the house.

. What is on the road to the shed?

_____

. What's **between** the house and fence on the **right**?

_____

. How many animals? _____

. Who is standing to the right of the pond? _____

Location and Map Reading

Here is a map of Our Town.
Find locations and plot a path.

N

SUNSHINE PARADE

SCHOOL

POST OFFICE

BANK

OVAL

PARK

ROAD

PATTERSON ROAD

HAWKE STREET

CHEMIST DOCTOR

THOMPSON

SUPERMARKET

FAIRFAX ROAD

PETROL

MILL STREET

CAR PARK

OWL AVENUE

HOSPITAL

POLICE STATION

BURMONT STREET

HOME

9. Plot this path from home -
   a. turn left along Burmont Street
   b. turn right into Thompson Road
   c. turn left into Hawke Street
   d. second business on the left.

   What am I _____

10. Name the roads running North, South.

    _____

11. What's on the corner of Thompson Road and Sunshine Parade?

    _____

12. What street is between the Police Station and Service Station?

    _____

13. Where can I find the church?

    _____

Fractions – Half and Symmetry

1. Colour half of each of these shapes.

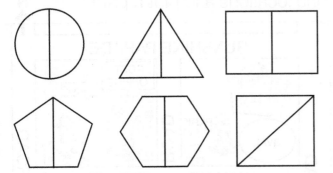

2. Colour the shapes that have symmetry.

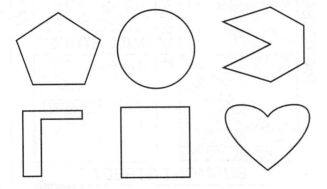

3. Draw the other half of these letters.

a. 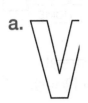 b.

c.  d.

4. Draw a line of symmetry.

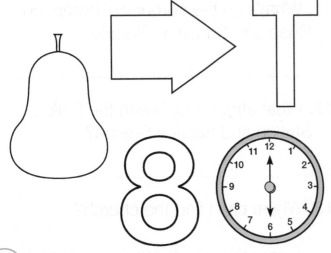

Half and Quarter

5. Colour the fraction of these shapes.

a. $\dfrac{1}{2}$ b. 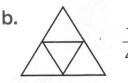 $\dfrac{1}{4}$

c. 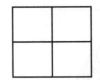 $\dfrac{1}{4}$ d. 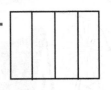 $\dfrac{3}{4}$

e. 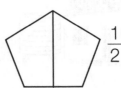 $\dfrac{1}{2}$ f. 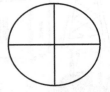 $\dfrac{3}{4}$

6. Colour the number of objects to match the fraction.

a.  $\dfrac{1}{2}$

b. 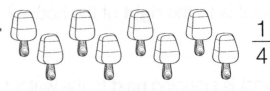 $\dfrac{3}{8}$

c. $\dfrac{1}{4}$

7. What fractional parts are shaded.

a.   b.   c.

_____   _____   _____

8. Colour half of each group and write how many.

a.  $\dfrac{1}{2}$ of 6 = ◯

b. $\dfrac{1}{2}$ of 10 = ◯

c. $\dfrac{1}{2}$ of 4 = ◯

New Syllabus Mentals and Extension 2, Stage C

. Tick which fraction is shaded on each shape.

a. $\frac{1}{2}$ ☐ $\frac{1}{4}$ ☐ $\frac{1}{8}$ ☐

b. 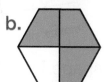 $\frac{1}{2}$ ☐ $\frac{1}{4}$ ☐ $\frac{3}{4}$ ☐

c. 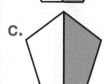 $\frac{1}{2}$ ☐ $\frac{1}{4}$ ☐ $\frac{1}{8}$ ☐

d.  $\frac{1}{2}$ ☐ $\frac{1}{4}$ ☐ $\frac{1}{8}$ ☐

. Colour one quarter of each group.

a.  b.

c. 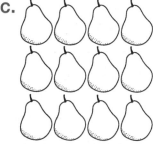 d.

. Divide this quadrilateral into 4 equal parts.

[ ]

. Colour the fractional part of each shape.

a.   b.   c.

$\frac{1}{4}$ $\frac{5}{8}$ $\frac{1}{4}$

d.  $\frac{3}{8}$

5. Write the fraction of the shaded part in each group. Count the parts first.

a.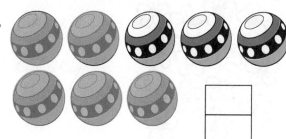

b.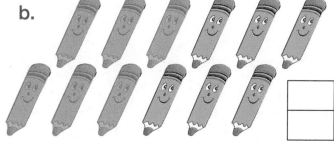

6. Colour the fraction for each shape.

a. $\frac{1}{4}$ b. $\frac{1}{2}$ c. $\frac{3}{4}$

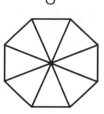

d. $\frac{1}{8}$ e. $\frac{3}{4}$ f. $\frac{3}{8}$

7. What fractional part is missing or gone from these.

a.  b.

c.   d.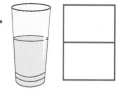

1. Colour the fractional part of each group.

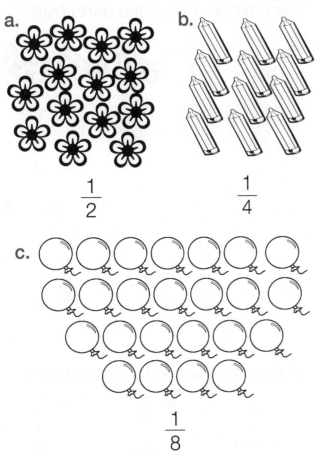

a.

b.

$\dfrac{1}{2}$ $\dfrac{1}{4}$

c.

$\dfrac{1}{8}$

2. What fraction in each groups in red?

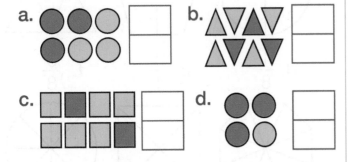

a.   b.

c.   d.

3. Count dots then complete sentences.

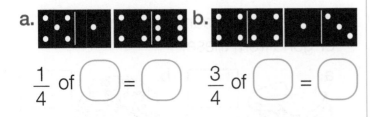

a.   b.

$\dfrac{1}{4}$ of ◯ = ◯ $\dfrac{3}{4}$ of ◯ = ◯

4. Divide each shape into four parts.

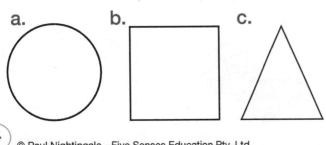

a.   b.   c.

5. Colour a quarter of these shapes or objects.

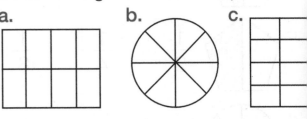

a.   b.   c.

6. Colour an eighth of each shape.

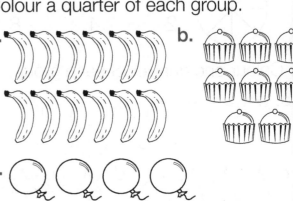

a.   b.   c.

7. Colour a quarter of each group.

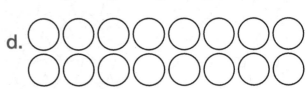

a.   b.

c.

d.

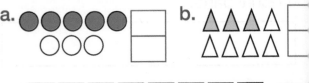
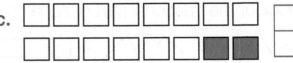

8. How many eighths in each group are coloured? Complete the fraction.

a.   b.

c.

9. Complete each fraction.

a. $\dfrac{1}{2}$ of 8 = ◯   b. $\dfrac{1}{4}$ of 4 = ◯

c. $\dfrac{1}{8}$ of 24 = ◯   d. $\dfrac{3}{8}$ of 16 = ◯

New Syllabus Mentals and Extension 2, Stage C

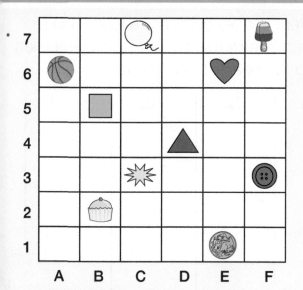

a. What can be found at E1? _____

b. What is at B2? _____

c. What is at C7? _____

d. Write the coordinates for the heart?

_____

. Write the fraction coloured for each shape.

a.  **b.** **c.**

d.  **e.**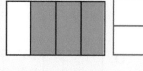

. Divide this shape into 8 equal parts.

. Tick the shape that is an eighth coloured.

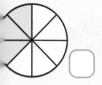 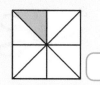

0. Write the fraction for these numbers.

a. Half of 8 = ◯ **b.** $\frac{1}{4}$ of 12 = ◯

2. a. What shape or object is right of the orange? _____

b. What shape is between the heart and cake? _____

c. What item is fifth? _____

d. What is left of the triangle? _____

3.

19	17	16	15	14
33	44	55	66	77
8	18	28	38	48
5	10	15	20	25

a. Number above 55? ◯

b. Number to the right of 38? ◯

c. Numbers below 66? ◯ ◯

5. Colour the shapes with symmetry.

7. What fraction of this shape is NOT coloured?

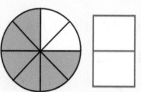

9. What fraction of each shape is shaded?

a. **b.** 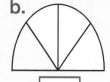 **c.**

Length - Metre

1. Here is a one metre rope with ribbon tied to it. Colour the ribbon that shows half a metre.

2. Here is a same rope. Colour the ribbon that shows three quarters of a metre.

3. Here is a metre rule. Estimate how many of your hand spans equals a metre.

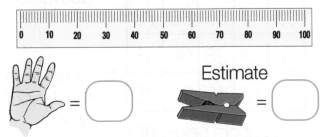

= ⬡   Estimate   = ⬡

4. Colour the measurement frame to estimate these to the nearest metre.

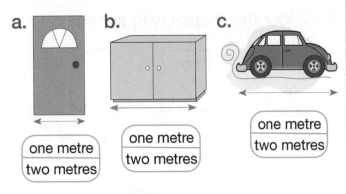

a.   one metre / two metres

b.   one metre / two metres

c.   one metre / two metres

5. Colour the objects smaller than a metre.

a.   **b.**   **c.**

d.   **e.**   **f.**

6. Tick the one that is about 100 metres.

Bus ⬡   Car ⬡   Train ⬡

Length - Centimetre

7. Here is a 30 centimetre ruler. Use a centimetre rule to measure these lines to the nearest centimetre.

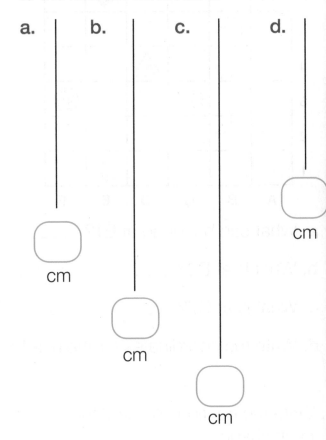

a.   **b.**   **c.**   **d.**

⬡ cm

⬡ cm

⬡ cm

⬡ cm

8. How many centimetres are each of these in length.

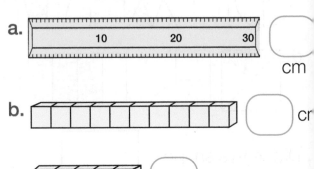

a.   10   20   30   ⬡ cm

b.   ⬡ cm

c.   ⬡ cm

9. Use a ruler to measure these.

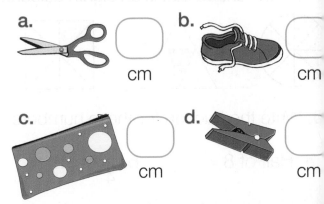

a.   ⬡ cm   **b.**   ⬡ cm

c.   ⬡ cm   **d.**   ⬡ cm

New Syllabus Mentals and Extension 2, Stage C

. Measure these objects in your kitchen with a ruler.

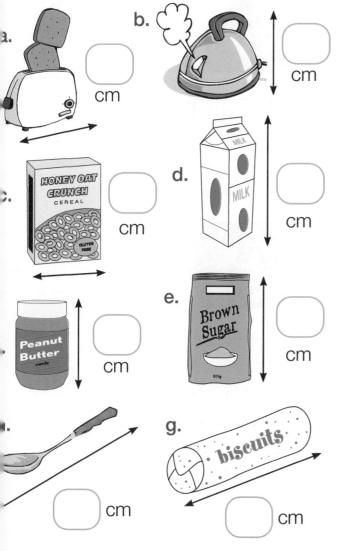

a. ○ cm

b. ○ cm

c. ○ cm

d. ○ cm

e. ○ cm

. ○ cm

g. ○ cm

. Measure these using your ruler.

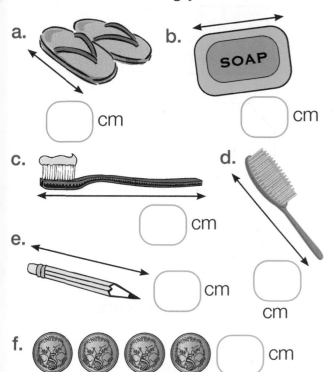

a. ○ cm

b. ○ cm

c. ○ cm

d. ○ cm

e. ○ cm

f. ○ cm

3. Use a ruler and to the nearest centimetre, find the length of each object.

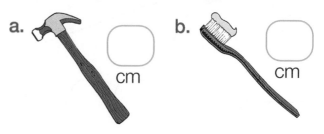

a. ○ cm

b. ○ cm

4. Measure the length of each MAB block with a ruler.

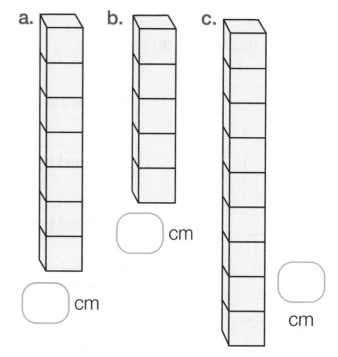

a. ○ cm

b. ○ cm

c. ○ cm

5. Use a ruler to measure each side of the triangle and quadrilaterals.

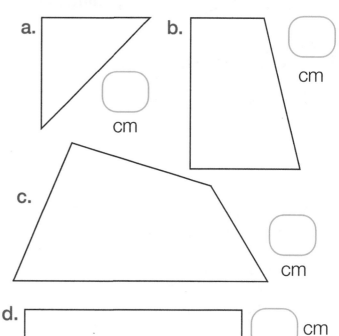

a. ○ cm

b. ○ cm

c. ○ cm

d. ○ cm

1. Draw an X on the **curved** lines.

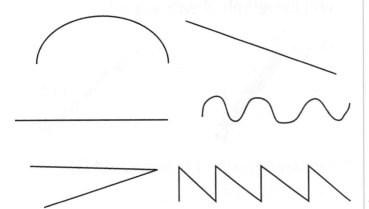

2. Match each line name

a.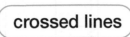

horizontal line

b.

crossed lines

curved line

c.

parallel lines

d.

broken line

e.

joining lines

3. Tick the open shapes - lines.

a.  **b.** **c.**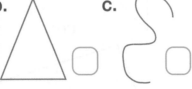

4. Add a line to make close shapes.
Colour them when closed.

a. **b.** **c.**

5. Name each 2D shape.

a.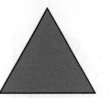

_____

b.

_____

c.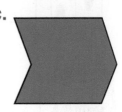

_____

d.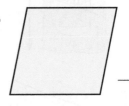

_____

e.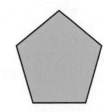

_____

f.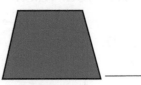

_____

g.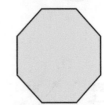

_____

h.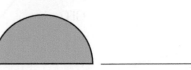

_____

6. Tick all the **quadrilaterals**.

7. How many shapes have
more than 4 angles? _____

. Count the edges and corners on each shape.

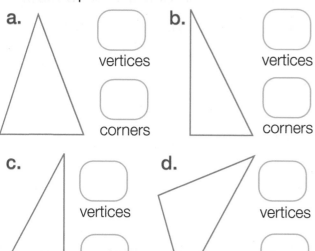

a. ⬜ vertices ⬜ corners

b. ⬜ vertices ⬜ corners

c. ⬜ vertices ⬜ corners

d. ⬜ vertices ⬜ corners

. Do all triangles have the same number of sides and angles? Yes ⬜ No ⬜

. Count the edges and corners on each shape.

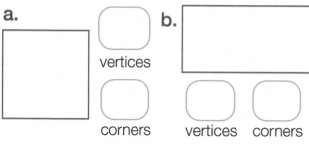

a. ⬜ vertices ⬜ corners

b. ⬜ vertices ⬜ corners

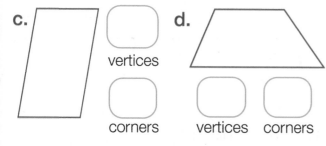

c. ⬜ vertices ⬜ corners

d. ⬜ vertices ⬜ corners

. Do all four sided shapes have 4 vertices? Yes ⬜ No ⬜

All 4 sided and 4 edged shapes are called quadrilaterals. 'quad' means 4 and 'tri' means 3

. Tick the quadrilaterals

 a.

 b.

 c.

Shapes with six sides and six corners are hexagons. Shapes with eight sides and eight corners are octagons.

6. Colour the hexagons.

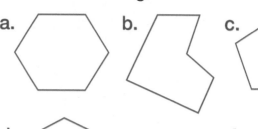

a.   b.   c.

d.   e.   f.

7. Join the dots to draw different shapes. Label each as hexagon or octagon.

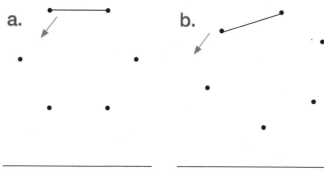

a.   b.

_____   _____

c.   d.

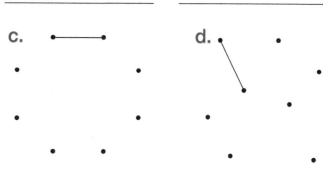

_____   _____

8. Colour the octagons.

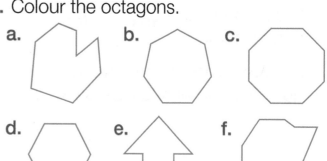

a.   b.   c.

d.   e.   f.

Rhombus and Trapezium

1. Colour the trapeziums yellow and the rhombuses blue.

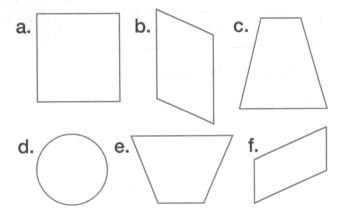

2. Join the dots starting at one to draw a rhombus or a trapezium. Name each shape. Use a ruler.

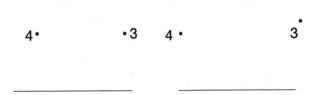

a. 1•   •2   **b.**   1•   •2

    4•   •3   4•   3•

    _____   _____

c. 1•   •2   **d.**   1•   •2

    4•   •3   4•   •3

    _____   _____

3. Is a trapezium a quadrilateral?   Yes ☐ No ☐

4. Is a rhombus a quadrilateral?   Yes ☐ No ☐

5. If a three sided figure is not a quadrilateral, what shape is it?

_____

6. What shape has only one side and no vertices? _____

Shapes and Patterns

7. Colour the hexagons red, octagons yellow and the quadrilaterals blue.

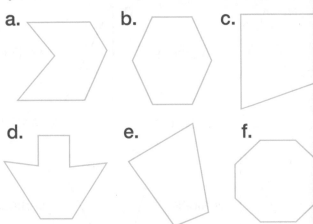

8. Continue the tile pattern. Use the dots. Colour it.

a.
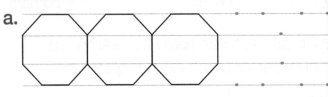

b.
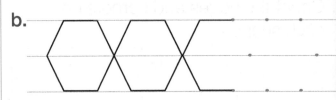

9. Colour the trapeziums.

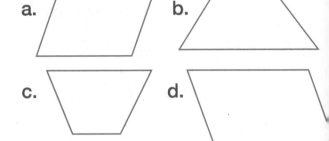

10. Name this shape.

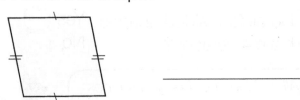

_____

11. Name this shape.

_____

. A door is higher in measurement than a metre.

Tick Yes ☐ or No ☐

. A car is about 4 metres long.

Tick True ☐ or False ☐

. How many centimetres in a quarter of a metre? ☐ cm

. Write the measurement of this line.

⟵───────────────⟶

☐ centimetres

. Name each of these 2D shapes.

a. ☐   b. ○   c. ◁

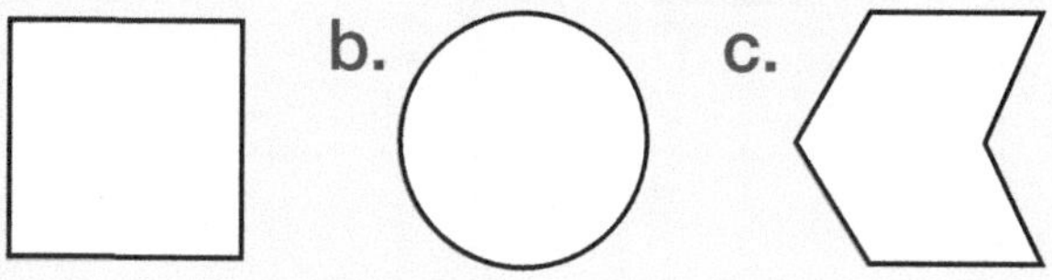

_____ _____ _____

1. How many edges and vertices on this shape?

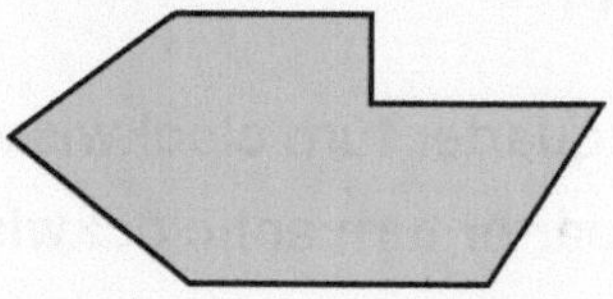

☐ vertices

☐ corners

3. Colour the quadrilaterals.

a.   b.   c.

d.   e.   f.

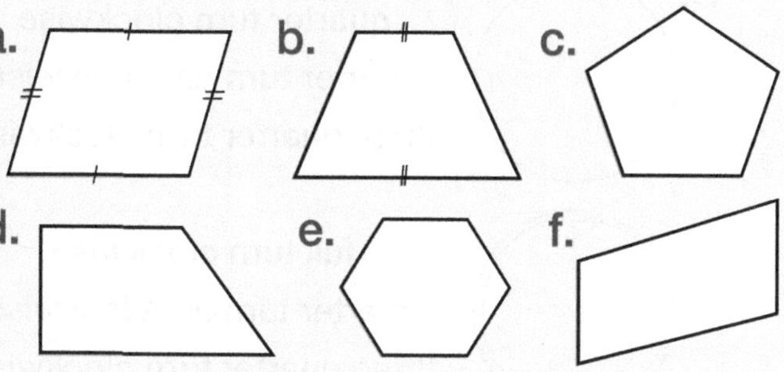

5. How many centimetres on each measurement?

a. 3 metres= _____ cm

b. 2½ metres= _____ cm

2. How many centimetres in one metre? ☐

4. If each block is one centimetre, how long is this row of blocks?

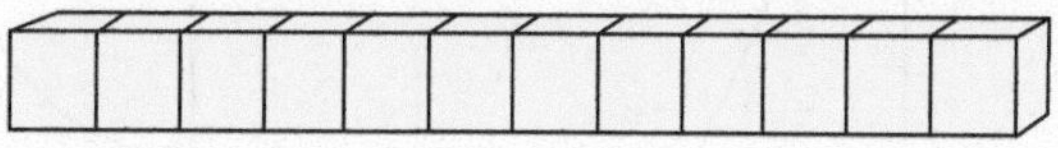

☐ cm

6. The length of a student ruler is 30 centimetres.

Tick True ☐ or False ☐

8. What type of line is this?

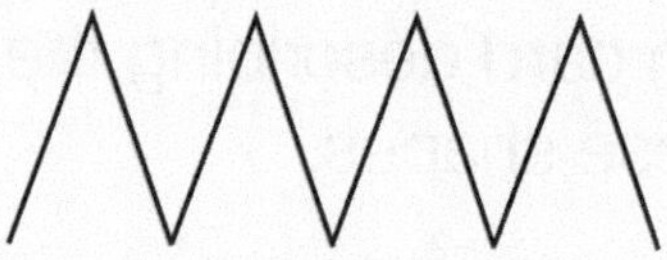

/\/\/\/\ _____

10. How many sides on a quadrilateral? ☐ sides

12. Colour the hexagons.

a.   b.   c.

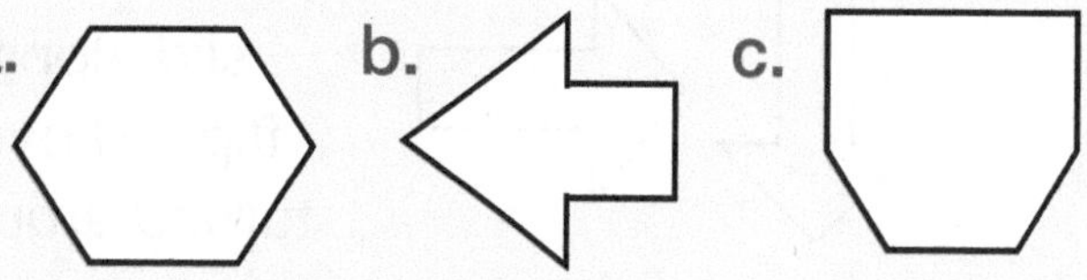

14. Name these shapes.

a.   b.

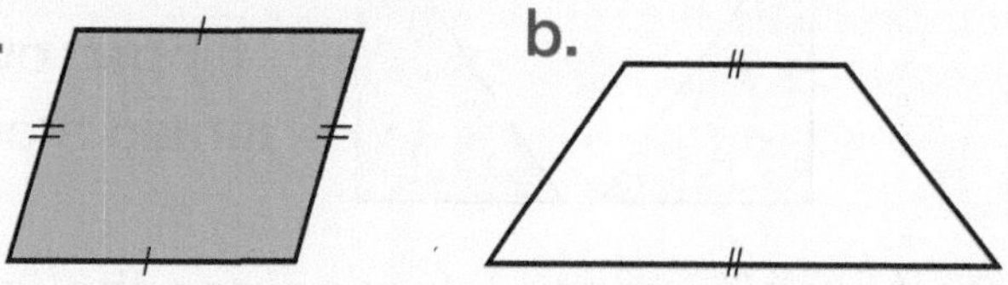

_____ _____

16. Join the dots to draw a shape, colour it red then name it.

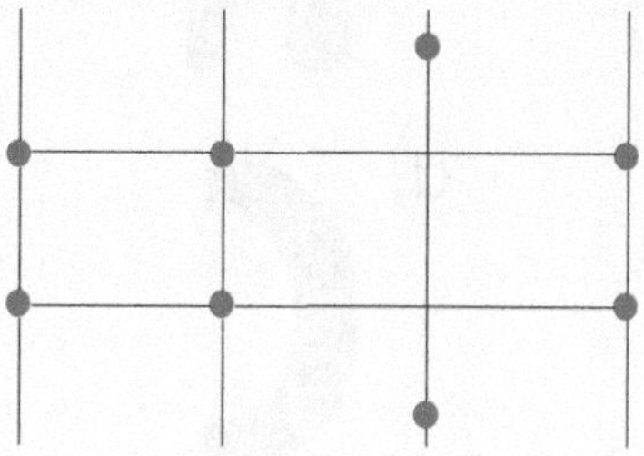

_____

1. Draw the shape you will see when each is **flipped** to the **left**.

a.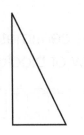

b.

c.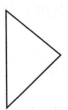

d.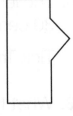

2. Colour the action card describing the movement of these shapes.

a.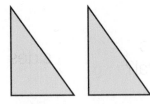

| slid along |
| flipped over |
| turned around |

b.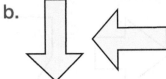

| slid along |
| flipped over |
| turned around |

c.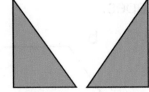

| slid along |
| flipped over |
| turned around |

3. If you flip these letter across the line of symmetry you can draw the other half.

a.

b.

c.

d.

4. Draw the shape you will see when each shape is **flipped downwards.**

a.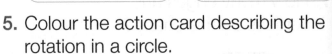

b.

c.

d.

5. Colour the action card describing the rotation in a circle.

a.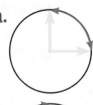

| quarter turn clockwise |
| quarter turn anticlockwise |
| three quarter turn clockwise |

b.

| quarter turn clockwise |
| quarter turn anticlockwise |
| three quarter turn clockwise |

c.

| full turn clockwise |
| quarter turn anticlockwise |
| three quarter turn clockwise |

6. How many quarter turns in one rotation?

◯ turns

7. How many quarter turns in a half rotation?

◯ turns

New Syllabus Mentals and Extension 2, Stage C

. Colour the shapes that have an area.

a. b. c.

d. e.

. Colour the shape with the **largest** area.

a. b.

c.

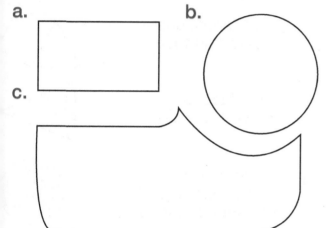

. Order the sizes of these envelopes, smallest to largest area, 1 to 5.

a. b.

c.

d. e.

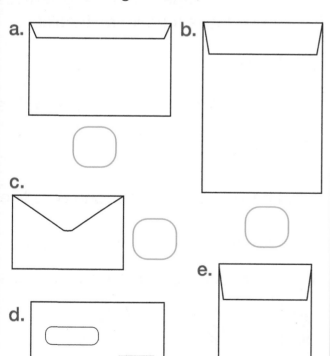

4. Count the squares in each shape. Write the totals then colour the middle sized area.

a. b.

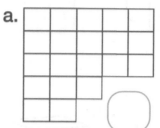

c.

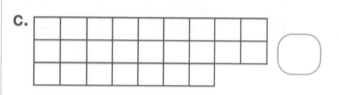

5. Which of these has the **largest** area.

_____ has the largest area.

6. Record the area for each of these shapes.

a.

squares

b.

triangles

c.

hexagons

1. Name each 3D solid, eg. pyramid.

a.   b.   c.

_____   _____   _____

d.   e.   f.

_____   _____   _____

2. Here are everyday objects we see. Write their 3D names.

a.   b.   c.

_____   _____   _____

d.   e.

_____   _____

3. Count the faces, vertices and edges on each 3D solid.

a.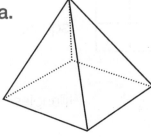
◯ faces
◯ vertices
◯ edges

b.
◯ faces
◯ vertices
◯ edges

4. Draw a line from each feature to the correct 3D object.

a. one curved surface

b. six equal faces

c. eight faces twelve vertices

d. two faces, one curved surface

e. one face, one curved surface

f. two triangular faces and three rectangular faces

5. What am I?

a. I have 12 edges, 6 faces, 8 vertices and 4 faces that are rectangles.

I am a _____

b. I have 9 edges, 5 faces and 6 vertices

I am a _____

c. I have 6 square faces and 8 vertices

I am a _____

6. Tick the objects with curved surfaces.

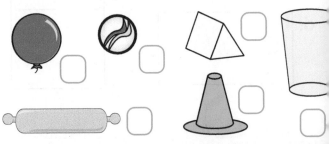

. Match the prisms to their nets.

a.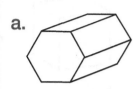

e.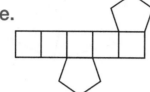

b.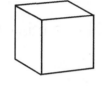

f.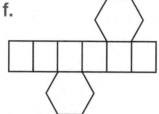

c.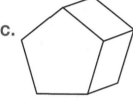

g.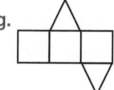

d.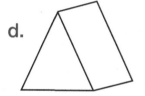

h.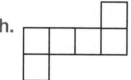

. Match each net to the object it will make.

a.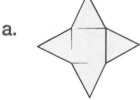

cylinder

b.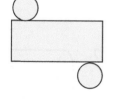

cube

c.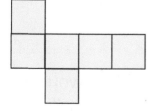

cone

d.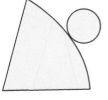

pyramid

3. Match each side view to its 3D solid.

a.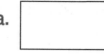

b.

c.

d.

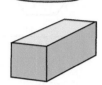

4. Match the shape you see when the 3D object is cut in half.

a.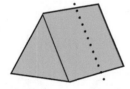

b.

c.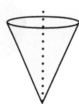

d.

5. A pyramid has these faces. How many edges? The answer is NOT 16.

 edges

55

1. Match each pyramid to its name.

a.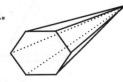

e. rectangular pyramid

b.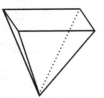

f. square pyramid

c.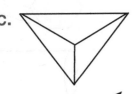

g. hexagonal pyramid

d.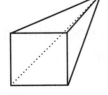

h. triangular pyramid

2. Tick the 3D objects that will sink.

3. Join the dots to draw a 3D solid. Label them.

a.    b.

c.

4. Name these solids.

a. 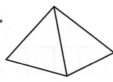   b.

_____   _____

5. How many faces on a brick?

6. Name this objec

_____

7. What am I?

I have 7 faces, 15 edges and 10 corner

I am a _____

8. Is a $1 coin a cylinder?

Tick Yes ☐ or No ☐

9. How many curved surfaces on this 3D object?

10. What shape is the icecream?

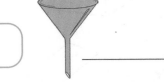

_____

11. Name these solids.

a. 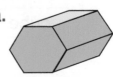   b.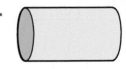

_____   _____

12. Colour the shape you would see when the cake is cut in half.

. Count and record the number of blocks in each solid.

a.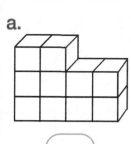

b.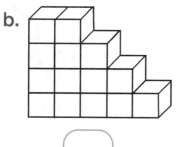

. Colour the object or shapes that have volume.

a.    b.

c.   d.   e.

. Count the blocks in each group.

a. 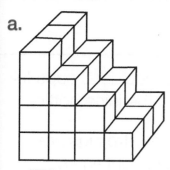   b.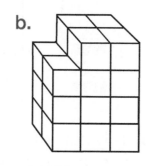

 Blocks    Blocks

c.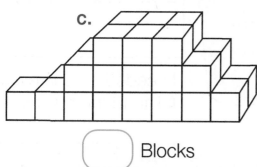

Blocks

. Order the volume of blocks **smallest** to **largest**, a to c.

1st   2nd   3rd

5. Count the blocks to measure the length, height and width.

a.   b.

Length   Length

Height   Height

Width   Width

6. Colour the **largest** solid.

7. To calculate volume of the solids above, multiply the length x height x width.

a. ☐ x ☐ x ☐ = ☐ blocks

b. ☐ x ☐ x ☐ = ☐ blocks

8. Count the blocks in each model.

a.   b.

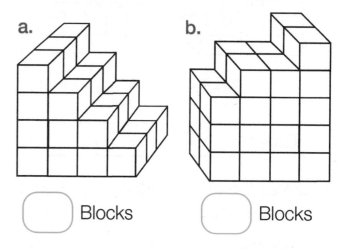

☐ Blocks   ☐ Blocks

9. Which model has the larger volume?

a ☐ or b ☐

10. Does a football have volume?

Yes ☐ or No ☐

Measuring Volume - Displacement

1. Colour the object that would make water in the jug rise the most.

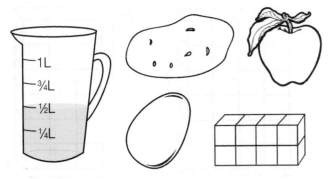

2. Complete the sentence.

The difference in water level is the

_____ of the object.

3. Count the blocks in each model then order them **smallest** to **largest** in volume.

a. ◯ Blocks

b. 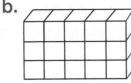 ◯ Blocks

c.  ◯ Blocks

d.  ◯ Blocks

Order [| | |]

4. Colour the objects water displacement could be used to measure volumes.

Plasticine

Capacity and Volume

5. Colour the objects that could hold things

6. Which container is most suitable to us to fill the bucket? Colour it.

7. Use the tally method to find how man cups full of water are needed to fill each container.

TALLY

I needed _____ cups full to fill the juice bottle.

8. Tally how many one litre jugs are needed to fill these containers.

a.

TALLY

I needed _____ litre jugs full to fill the bucket.

b.

TALLY

I needed _____ litre jugs full to fill the ice cream container.

New Syllabus Mentals and Extension 2, Stage C

One Litre (L) is a formal unit of measurement for capacity. Milk, petrol and water are measured in litres (L).

. Write the unit of measurement for the capacity of these objects.

a.

b.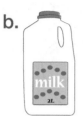

c.

9 _____   2 _____   300 _____

d.

e.

60 _____   1500 _____

. List containers in the house that hold more than 1L and less than 1L.

More than 1L	Less than 1L
_____	_____
_____	_____
_____	_____

. Tick the objects that will stack.

4. Different containers were used to fill a small bucket. The tally method was used to count the number of fills. Write the number used for each container.

a.

b.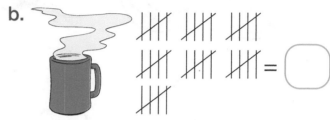

c.

5. Colour the most suitable container used to fill the esky.

6. Check capacity then order these containers 1-7 **largest** to **smallest**.

Comparing Mass

Mass is the amount of solid in an object that we often call weight.

1. Compare these objects then order their mass 1-6 **lightest** to **heaviest**.

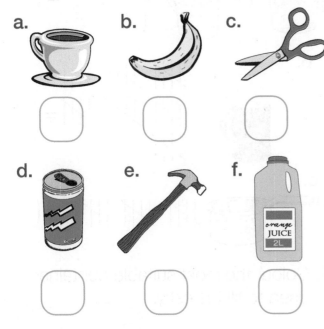

a. ☐ b. ☐ c. ☐

d. ☐ e. ☐ f. ☐

2. Colour the one with the **smallest** mass. Use hefting to help your selection.

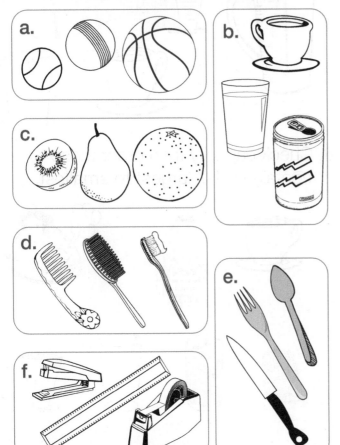

Measuring Mass

3. Use an equal arm balance or dish scale to measure and compare mass.

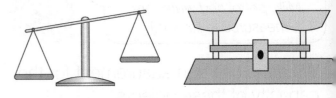

Colour the **larger** mass item.

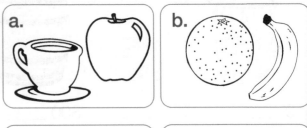

a. b.

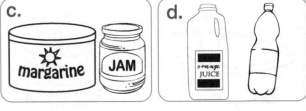

c. d.

e. f.

4. Circle the action of each balance beam when marbles are added or taken away.

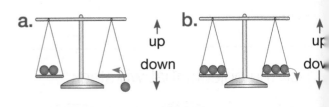

a. up down   b. up dow

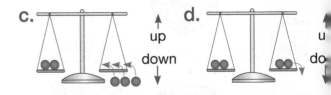

c. up down   d. u do

5. Tick the objects that have a mass **less than** a brick.

New Syllabus Mentals and Extension 2, Stage C

. Using kitchen scales find the **heavier** one in each group. Colour it.

Draw a line from each object to where it fits best to match the scales.

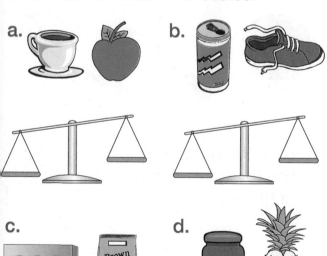

3. Use kitchen or balance scales to find if the item is equal to, less than or greater than one kilogram. Colour the path.

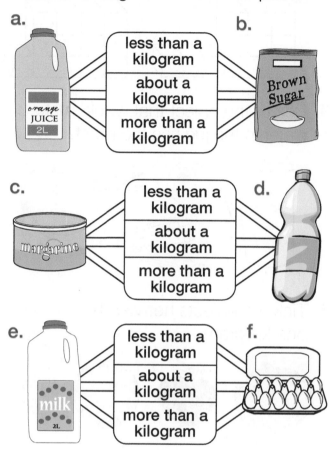

4. List three things lighter and three things heavier than each item.

lighter		heavier

5. Order the mass of these 1 to 5. Lightest first.

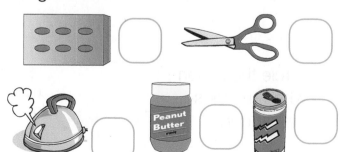

1. Colour the blocks with the larger volume.

a. 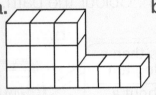 b.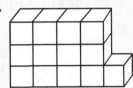

2. Tick the objects that have volume.

3. Colour the object that would make water in the jug rise the **most**.

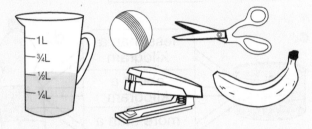

4. Tick the object that would need displacement method to find volume.

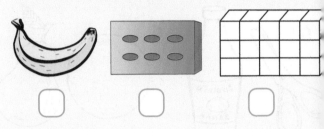

5. Tick the objects **heavier** than one kilogram.

6. Colour the best container to use to fill the bucket.

7. What numbers are shown by these tally marks?

a. 𝍷𝍷𝍷𝍷 𝍷𝍷𝍷𝍷 𝍷𝍷𝍷𝍷 𝍷𝍷𝍷𝍷 || = ◯

b. 𝍷𝍷𝍷𝍷 𝍷𝍷𝍷𝍷 𝍷𝍷𝍷𝍷 𝍷𝍷𝍷𝍷 𝍷𝍷𝍷𝍷 | = ◯

8. Tick the **lightest** object.

9. Order the mass of these four items.

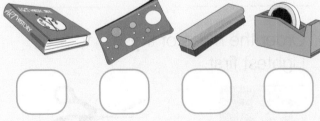

◯ ◯ ◯ ◯

10. Fill in the numbers to find the total number of blocks.

◯ X ◯ X ◯ = ◯

blocks

11. Circle the action when marbles are added.

up
down

12. If a brick has a mass of 2 kilograms, what it the mass of 7 bricks?

◯ kilograms

New Syllabus Mentals and Extension 2, Stage

Days, Dates and Months

. Write the days of the week in order alongside the ordinal numbers.

1st _____ 2nd _____

3rd _____ 4th _____

5th _____ 6th _____

. Write the number of days in each of these months.

November ◯   August ◯

March ◯   January ◯

April ◯   September ◯

. How many months of the year have thirty-one days? ◯ months

. Write the seasons for these months.

a. [September   October   November]

_____

b. [March   April   May]

_____

. Write the months of winter.

_____ _____ _____

. How many days in winter? ◯ days

. Write the months **before** and **after**.

a. _____ June _____

b. _____ January _____

c. _____ August _____

. How many days in spring? ◯ days

Calendar for April

Here is a calendar for the month of April.

S	M	T	W	T	F	S
APRIL						
				1	2	3
4	5	6	7	8	9	10
11	12	13	14	15	16	17
18	19	20	21	22	23	24
25	26	27	28	29	30	

9. What day and date is April Fool's Day?

_____ _____

10. What day and date is Anzac Day?

_____ _____

11. On what day will 1st May occur?

_____

12. What are the dates of the **first** weekend in April?

_____ _____

13. In what season is April?

_____

14. How many days from 8th April until 21st April? ◯ days

15. How many months in the year with 30 days? ◯ months

16. On what day is the last day of March? _____

17. How many weekends in April? ◯

63

Calendar for June

Here is a calendar for the month of June. It is not this year's calendar.

JUNE						
S	**M**	**T**	**W**	**T**	**F**	**S**
			1	2	3	4
5	6	7	8	9	10	11
12	13	14	15	16	17	18
19	20	21	22	23	24	25
26	27	28	29	30		

1. What day was 31st May? _____

2. What are the dates for the last weekend in June? _____ _____

3. Write the day and date for the day after the last day of June.

   _____

4. Is there usually a long weekend in June?

   Yes ⬭ No ⬭

5. If so, write the days and dates.

   Days   Dates

   _____   _____

   _____   _____

   _____   _____

6. What other months have 30 days?

   _____

   _____

   _____

7. In what season does June occur? _____

Winter Months

Here is a calendar for winter. It is not this year's calendar.

June													
S	M	T	W	T	F	S	S	M	T	W	T	F	S
				1	2	3	4	5	6	7	8	9	10
11	12	13	14	15	16	17	18	19	20	21	22	23	24
25	26	27	28	29	30								

July													
S	M	T	W	T	F	S	S	M	T	W	T	F	S
							1	2	3	4	5	6	7	8
9	10	11	12	13	14	15	16	17	18	19	20	21	22
23	24	25	26	27	28	29	30	31					

August													
S	M	T	W	T	F	S	S	M	T	W	T	F	S
									1	2	3	4	5
6	7	8	9	10	11	12	13	14	15	16	17	18	19
20	21	22	23	24	25	26	27	28	29	30	31		

8. On what day of the week does winter finish? _____

9. What day is 1st July? _____

10. What are the dates for the first weekend in winter?

    _____   _____

11. What is the day and date for the last day of autumn?

    _____   _____

12. How many Saturdays in July? ⬭

13. What are the dates for the last weekend in winter?

    _____   _____

14. How many days in winter? ⬭

15. Do you like winter? Yes ⬭ No ⬭

Duration of Time

. Tick the pictures that would take five minutes or less to do.

a.　　　　b.　　　　c.

. Tick the duration of time for these activities to happen.

a.
- ◯ 10 minutes
- ◯ 1 hour
- ◯ 1 day

b.
- ◯ 10 minutes
- ◯ 1 hour
- ◯ 1 day

. Tick the sunrise picture.

a.　　　b.　　　c.　　　d.

◯　　◯　　◯　　◯

. Colour the box to show how long it would take to do these things.

- ◯ 1 day
- ◯ 2 days
- ◯ 6 minutes
- ◯ 6 hours

. How many days in these seasons?

a.  ☐ days

b.  ☐ days

---

Time to the Quarter Hour

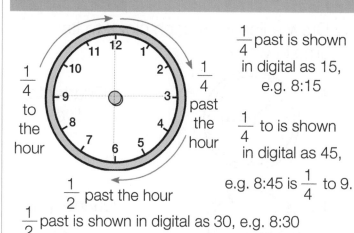

$\frac{1}{4}$ to the hour

$\frac{1}{4}$ past the hour

$\frac{1}{4}$ past is shown in digital as 15, e.g. 8:15

$\frac{1}{4}$ to is shown in digital as 45, e.g. 8:45 is $\frac{1}{4}$ to 9.

$\frac{1}{2}$ past the hour

$\frac{1}{2}$ past is shown in digital as 30, e.g. 8:30

6. Write each time in digital form.

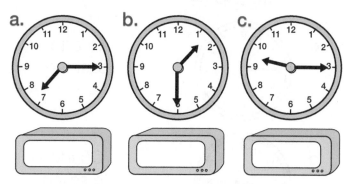

a.　　　　b.　　　　c.

7. Show each time on the clock face.

a. $\frac{1}{4}$ past 3　　b. $\frac{1}{4}$ to 9　　c. $\frac{1}{4}$ past 6

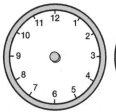  

d. $\frac{1}{4}$ to 4　　e. $\frac{1}{4}$ past 8　　f. $\frac{1}{4}$ to 7

  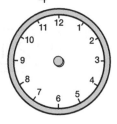

8. What time is showing on each clock?

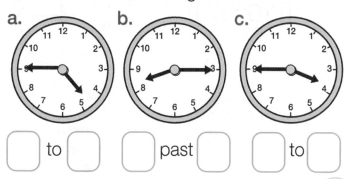

a.　　　　b.　　　　c.

☐ to ☐　　☐ past ☐　　☐ to ☐

65

1. Draw a line from each clock to its time in words.

a.

Quarter to five

b.

Quarter past eight

c.

Quarter past ten

d.

Quarter to seven

2. Match the digital time to the clock with the matching time.

a. 6:45

e.

b. 12:15

f.

c. 10:45

g.

d. 1:15

h.

3. Show these times on each clock face.

a.  b. c.

half past four   quarter past seven   quarter to three

d. e. f.

quarter to nine   quarter past eight   nine o'clock

4. Draw a line to match the same digital and clock face times.

a. 6:15

A.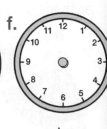

b. 2:45

B.

c. 4:45

C.

d. 8:30

D.

5. Write these times as 'quarter to' or a 'quarter past'.

a. 10:45 _____

b. 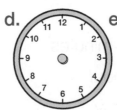 _____

c. 8:15

New Syllabus Mentals and Extension 2, Stage C

Analogue and Digital Time

. Show the time on the clock face.

a. quarter past six

b. quarter past nine

c. quarter past two

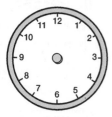

d. quarter to five

e. quarter to three

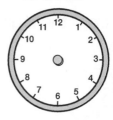

f. quarter to four

. Draw a line from each digital time to that time in words.

a. 7:45   Quarter past eight

b. 3:15   Quarter to seven

c. 6:45   Quarter past three

d. 8:15   Quarter to three

e. 10:15   Quarter to eight

f. 2:45   Quarter to ten

. What time is shown on each clock face?

a.

b.

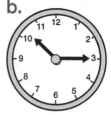

c.

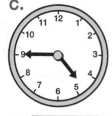

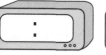

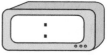

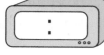

Time – Quarter and Quarter Past

4. Write the time in digital form.

a. half past six

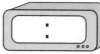

b. quarter past two

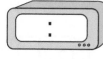

c. quarter to five

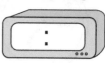

d. quarter past eight

e. half past nine

f. quarter to seven

5. Write the time in words.

a.

 _____

b.

 _____

c.

 _____

d.

 _____

e.

_____

6. Match each event to the best time.

a.

7:30

6:30

2:00

10:30

b.

c.

d.

Analogue and Digital Time

1. Match the analogue and digital times.

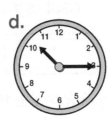

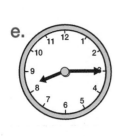

2. Write the time in words.

a. 5:45 _____

b. 6:15 _____

c. _____

d. 8:15 _____

3. Write the time in digital format.

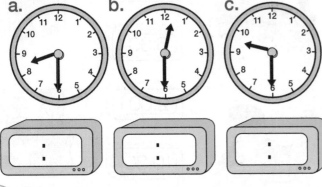

a.   b.   c.

Time To and From the Hour

4. Write the time on the clock face in digital time.

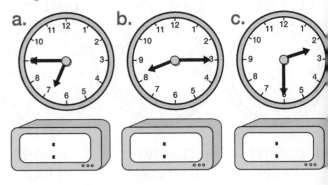

a.   b.   c.

5. Draw a line from the digital time to the written time.

a. 7:45   Quarter to
                           seven

b. 3:15   Quarter past
                           eight

c. 6:45   Quarter to
                           eight

d. 8:15   Quarter past
                           three

6. Draw a minute and an hour hand on each clock face to show the time.

a. 11:15   b. 3:15   c. 2:45

d. 6:00   e. 8:15   f. 9:45

7. What time do you have dinner at home?

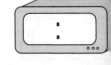

New Syllabus Mentals and Extension 2, Stage

1. How many days in September? ◯

2. What is the eighth month of the year? _____

3. What date is ANZAC Day?

_____

4. Name the autumn months.

_____ _____ _____

5. How long does it take to eat your lunch? Tick you estimate of time.

◯ five minutes   ◯ half an hour   ◯ two hours

6.  Write this time in words.

_____

7. Fill in the digital time to match the analogue clock.

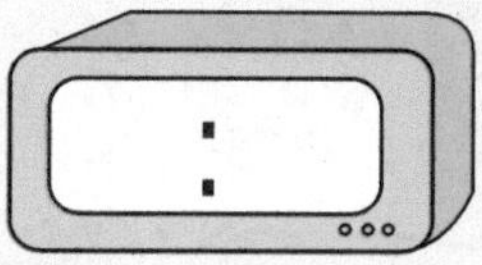

8. Write this time in words.

3:15

_____
_____

9. Draw hands on the clock to show a quarter to ten.

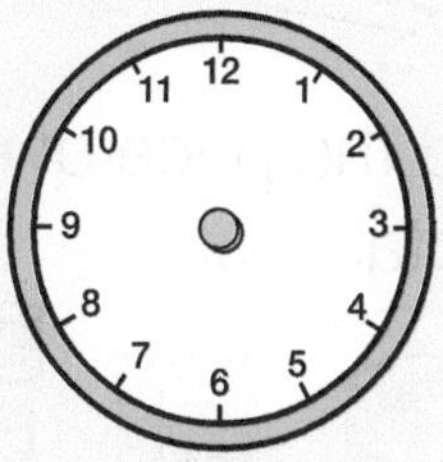

10. Write the digital time for a quarter past six.

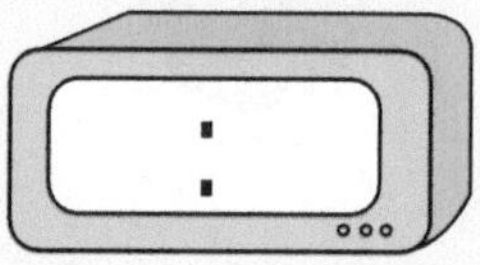

11. Write a quarter to nine in digital form.

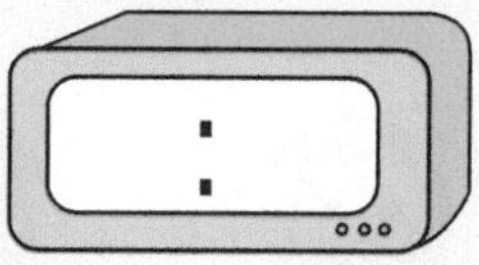

12. What time is shown on this analogue clock.

_____
_____

13. Write this time in words.

2:45

_____
_____

14. How many minutes in half an hour? ◯ minutes

15. How many minutes in a quarter of an hour? ◯ minutes

16. Tick the time you go to school.

5:15   3:30

◯   ◯   ◯   ◯

17. Write the time on the digital clock when you go to bed.

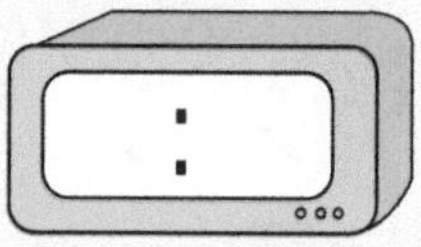

18. How many minutes in three quarters of an hour? ◯ minutes

19. Add hands to the clock to show a quarter to twelve.

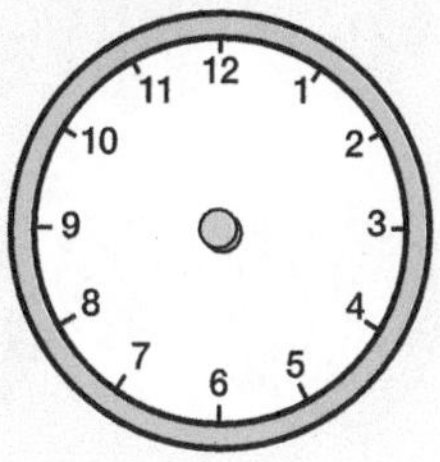

1. Name these coins.

a. _____

b. _____

c. _____

d.  _____

2. Order these coins in value, the **largest** first.

3. What is the value of each coin group?

a. = ⟨ o ⟩

b.  = ⟨ o ⟩

c. = ⟨ o ⟩

d. = ⟨ o ⟩

4. Colour the coins needed to buy these.

a.  $4.35

b.  $3.75

c.  $2.30

5. Add the price of each item and write a total cost.

a.  $2 $3 $9 $2 = $ _____

b.  $3 $3 $4 = $ _____

c.  $8 $7 $12 $9 = $ _____

6. Round these prices off to the nearest 5 cents.

a. ⟨ o 97c ⟩ _____   b. ⟨ o 88c ⟩ _____

c. ⟨ o 49c ⟩ _____   d. ⟨ o 52c ⟩ _____

New Syllabus Mentals and Extension 2, Stage (

. Name each coin.

a.
> I have five kangaroos
> on one side of me.
> I am the largest gold
> coin in size.

_____

b.
> I am a silver coin with
> a platypus swimming
> down the face.
> You need five of me
> to equal one dollar.

_____

c.
> I am the largest value
> silver coin with twelve
> edges and you need
> four of me to equal
> two dollars.

_____

. Round these prices up or down to
the nearest 5 cents.

a. 58c [   ] cents

b. 31c [   ] cents

c. 63c [   ] cents

d. 67c [   ] cents

e. 98c [   ] cents

f. 84c [   ] cents

Add each group of coins.

   = [   ]

   = [   ]

   = [   ]

4. What are the real prices for these items.

a.  $3.87 Real Price $ [   ]

b.  $3.77 Real Price $ [   ]

c.  $4.36 Real Price $ [   ]

d.  $3.99 Real Price $ [   ]

5. Calculate the change for the purchases
when coins are used.

a.  $1.00 Change [   ]

b.  $3.75 Change [   ]

c.  $5.90 Change [   ]

d.  $1.25 Change [   ]

e.  $2.65 Change [   ]

f.  $1.10 Change [   ]

6. Colour the correct card for each
money problem.

a.  | is equal to / not equal to | 50 cents

b.  | is equal to / not equal to | three dollars

1. Match each note to its value.

a.

    five dollars

b.

    ten dollars

c.

    twenty dollars

d.

    fifty dollars

e.

    one hundred dollars

2. Order the Australian notes from lowest to highest in value.

$	$	$	$	$

3. How many five dollar notes needed to equal these?

a.  b.  c.

( ) ( ) ( )

4. How many ten dollar notes needed to equal these?

a.  b.

( ) ( )

c.   ( )

5. Write the value of these coins and notes in words.

a.  _____

b.  _____

c. _____

d.  _____

e. _____

f. _____

g. _____

6. Write the total value in each group of coins and notes.

a.    = $ _____

b.     = $ _____

7. Mum gave me $10 pocket money. I already had $15.

How much do I have now?

$ ( ) + $ ( ) = $ ( )

New Syllabus Mentals and Extension 2, Stage

Money Notes and Coins Together

. Write the total of each group of coins and notes.

a.  = $ _____

b.  = $ _____

c.  = $ _____

. Add the value of notes and coins in each group.

 = $ _____

 = $ _____

 = $ _____

. Order from **highest to lowest** value the coins and notes.

Know Notes and Coins

4. Colour the notes, then count the amount of money in each group.

a.  = $ _____

b. 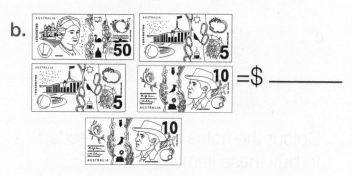 = $ _____

5. Colour the notes and coins needed to buy each item?

a.

b.

6. Add the notes and write the total amount.

a.  = $ _____

b.  = $ _____

1. How much money in each group?

a.  = $ _____

b.  = $ _____

c.  = $ _____

2. Colour the notes and coins needed to buy these items.

a.

$14.50

b.

$32.60

3. Add these sums of money.

a.  = $ _____

b.  = $ _____

4. Add each set of notes and coins

a.  = $ _____

b.  = $ _____

5. Write each amount.

a. $\frac{1}{2}$ of $20 ⬜   b. $\frac{1}{2}$ of $50 ⬜

c. $\frac{1}{4}$ of $20 ⬜   d. $\frac{3}{4}$ of $20 ⬜

e. $\frac{1}{2}$ of $100 ⬜   f. $\frac{1}{4}$ of $80 ⬜

6. Colour the Tap 'n' Go card.

7. Tick what can be bought using a Tap 'n' Go card.

⬜   ⬜   ⬜   ⬜

8. How old must you be to own a Tap 'n' Go card? ⬜ years old

9. Can you spend $100 using a Tap 'n' Go card? Tick Yes or No.

⬜ Yes
⬜ No

New Syllabus Mentals and Extension 2, Stage

1. What coin has platypus on one side?

_____

2. Name this coin.

_____

3. How many 5 cent coins are equal to 25 cents? ◯

4. What is the total of these coins? ◯

5. What coin am I?

I am a silver coin with a lyrebird on one side and I am an even number. ◯ cents

6. How many ten cents are equal to $2.50? ◯

7. Round each price up or down to the nearest five cents.

a. 67 cents = ◯ cents

b. 84 cents = ◯ cents

c. 62 cents = ◯ cents

8. Colour the correct path for these coins.

is equal to

not equal to

9. Write the name of this note in words.

_____

_____

10. Write the colour of each note.

a. $10 _____ b. $20 _____

c. $100 _____ d. $50 _____

11. What note am I?

I have a sailing boat and a colonial house on one side. Mary Reiby can be found on me. I am red in colour. $ _____

12. How many ten dollar notes are equal to one hundred dollars? ◯

13. Add these coins and notes.

$ _____

14. A kettle had a price of $29.75. If I gave the shop keeper a $50 note what change should I receive? $ _____

15. Can I buy an icecream with a Tap 'n' Go card? Tick Yes or No.

◯ Yes

◯ No

16. Write the order of coins **smallest** to **largest** in value.

◯ ◯ ◯ ◯ ◯

17. What is the value of Australia's **largest** note? _____

This graph shows student's favourite fruit.

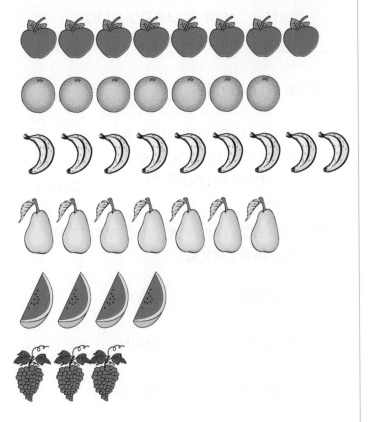

1. What fruit is most popular? _____

2. How many students like oranges? ◯

3. Which fruit is **least** popular? _____

4. How many more students like apples than watermelon? ◯

5. Which two fruits are equally popular?

   _____ _____

6. How many students like pears? ◯

7. What is the difference in popularity with bananas and grapes? ◯

8. Which fruit do you like best? ◯

9. How many students are represented on the graph? ◯

Here is a graph showing Pets at Home for students in Year 2 at My Town School.

10. What is the most popular pet? ____

11. How many students have a dog? ◯

12. Which pet is **least** popular? _____

13. How many more cats than turtles? ◯

14. How many students had chickens? ◯

15. How many more dogs than horses? ◯

16. What is your favourite pet? _____

17. How many pets altogether? ◯

18. What pet do you have or would like to have? _____

Tallying and Interpreting Data

Here is a tally record showing students' favourite colours.

Colour	Tallies	Totals
BLUE	IIII IIII II	
YELLOW	IIII III	
GREEN	IIII IIII I	
BLACK	IIII I	
ORANGE	IIII II	
RED	IIII IIII IIII	

Write the total for each colour.

What is the **most** popular colour on the graph? _____

How many students picked blue?

What is the **least** popular colour on the graph? _____

What is the **second most** popular colour? _____

How many **more** students chose blue than yellow?

How many **more** liked green than orange?

What is the total number of students who chose a colour?

What are your two favourite colours?

_____ _____

Comparing Data in a Column Graph

Look at the column graph about Year 2's favourite subjects, then answer the questions.

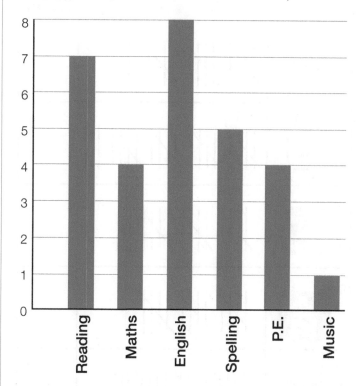

10. What is the **most** popular subject? _____

11. How many students like maths?

12. How many **more** students like reading than spelling?

13. Which is the **least** popular subject? _____

14. What subjects scored **equally** on the graph?

_____ _____

15. How many students like spelling?

16. How many more liked reading than music?

17. How many students in Year 2?

18. What is your favourite subject?

_____

© Paul Nightingale - Five Senses Education Pty. Ltd.

Here is a graph using tallies to count items on the shop's shelves.

TOTAL

a. biscuits	卌 卌 卌 I	
b.	卌 卌 卌 卌 III	
c. FLOUR	卌 卌 卌 III	
d. Jam	卌 卌 卌	
e. Peanut Butter	卌 卌 卌 III	

1. Count the tally for each item.

Remember I =1 II =2 III =3 IIII =4 卌 =5

2. Which item has **most** on the shelves? _____

3. Which item has **least** on the shelves? _____

4. Which two items have the **same** amount on the shelves?

_____ _____

5. How many **more** tomato sauce bottles are there than jam? _____

6. Of all the items which one do you like the **most**?

_____

Each student received stars for homewo[r]
Look at each tally and make a graph by colouring a square for each star.

Rhani 卌 卌 II Eli 卌 III Jon 卌 III Paris 卌 II

Josie 卌 卌 Samira 卌 卌 I Li 卌 卌 III Kim 卌

TOTAL

		TOTAL
Rhani	☐☐☐☐ ☐☐☐☐	
Eli	☐☐☐☐ ☐☐☐☐	
Jon	☐☐☐☐ ☐☐☐☐	
Paris	☐☐☐☐ ☐☐☐☐	
Josie	☐☐☐☐ ☐☐☐☐	
Samira	☐☐☐☐ ☐☐☐☐	
Li	☐☐☐☐ ☐☐☐☐	
Kim	☐☐☐☐ ☐☐☐☐	

7. Write the totals.

8. How many stars for Li? ☐

9. How many stars for Josie? ☐

10. Who has the **most** number of stars?

_____

11. Who has the **least** number of stars?

_____

12. How many **more** stars does Rhani have than Paris? ☐

13. How many stars do the girls have altogether? (Kim is a boy) ☐

14. How many stars do the boys have? ☐

15. How many stars do the eight students have in total? ☐

New Syllabus Mentals and Extension 2, Stage [

. Colour the chance card for each picture.

a.

I go to school by bus

likely
unlikely

b.

I will watch TV tonight.

likely
unlikely

c.

Sleep in my bed.

likely
unlikely

d.

Rain today.

likely
unlikely

e.

A sunny day tomorrow.

likely
unlikely

f.

Ride an elephant

likely
unlikely

Tick the activities that would be **impossible** to happen.

a.

Fly to the moon

b.

Duck driving train

c.

Ride my bike

d.

Pig flying

3. Roll a dice twenty times. Each time a number comes up draw it on a dice.

4. Organise the dice results into a graph using the tally method. Write totals.

Dice	Tally	Total
⚀		
⚁		
⚂		
⚃		
⚄		
⚅		

5. Which number came up the most?

6. Did 5 come up 6 times or more?_____

7. How many times did 4 turn up?

8. Did any faces turn up equally?_____

9. What were they? _____

10. What number turned up the least?

11. Would you get the same result if you threw the dice 20 more times? _____

12. Is there any certainty in a game of chance? Tick ☐ Yes ☐ No

1. Which is **most likely** to be picked from each 'feely' bag?

a.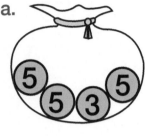

b.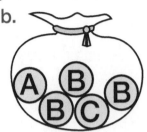

_____   _____

c.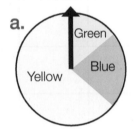

d.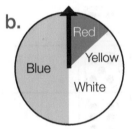

_____   _____

2. On which colour is each spinner **likely** to land?

a.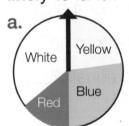

b.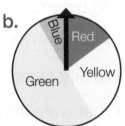

_____   _____

3. On which colour is the spinner **least likely** to land?

a.   b.

_____   _____

4. What is your chance of rolling a 6 with the dice? Colour the card.

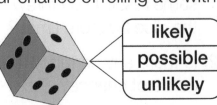

| likely |
| possible |
| unlikely |

5. Here is a box of letters. One letter is taken out. Which is **likely** to be picked

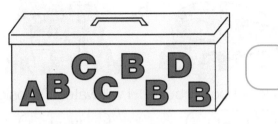

6. Here is a bag of coloured counters. If 2 were picked out together colour the possibility chance card.

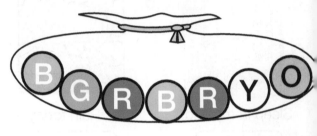

a. Two red counters
| possible |
| impossible |

b. Two green counters
| possible |
| impossible |

c. A blue and red counter
| possible |
| impossible |

7. Roll a dice 20 times and record the results. Use the tally method.

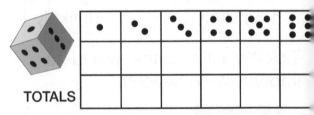

	•	••	•••	::	:::	:::
TOTALS						

a. Which number showed up the **most**?

b. Which number turned up the **least**?

c. Did any number turn up **more** than 7 times?

d. If you rolled 20 more times would you get the same result?

 Yes

 No

New Syllabus Mentals and Extension 2, Stage

p4

1.a. 34 b. 52 c. 75 d. 83
2.a. 44 b. 54 c. 46
3.a. 55 b. 29 c. 99 4.a. 47 b. 61 c. 32 d. 56
5. 37 thirty-seven, 52 fifty-two, 83 eighty-three, 49 forty-nine, 17 seventeen.
6.a. 28-30 b. 49-51 c. 63-65 d. 69-71
   e. 34-36 f. 97-99
7.a. 40 b. 60 c. 30
8.a. 25 b. 21   9. 9, 12, 18, 33, 52, 74

p5

1.a. 96 b. 57 c. 61 d. 25 e. 35 f. 43
2.a. 8 tens 4 ones b. 7 tens 2 ones
   c. 2 tens 5 ones d. 4 tens 9 ones
3.a. 90, 91, 92 b. 60, 55, 50 c. 60, 70, 80
   d. 18, 15, 12 e. 30, 32, 34
4.a. is larger than b. is larger than
5.a. 10,12_16 b. 42,44_48 c. 86,64_80
6. 5, 10, 15, 20, 25 7. 5, 10, 15, 20, 25, 35, 40
8.a. 20 b. 40 c. 45 d. 72
9.a. 45 b. 70 c. 75 d. 33
10.a. 2→ 4→ 6→ 8→ 10→ 12→ 14 Rule +2
    b. 5→ 10→ 15→ 20→ 25→ 30→ 35→ 40
    Rule +5   11. 25 cents

p6

1. 10, 20, 30, 40, 50, 60, 70
2.a. 8 tens 2 ones, 84 b. 7 tens 3 ones, 73
3.a. 16, 18, 20, 22, 24 b. 40, 50, 60 c. 94, 92, 90
4.a. 50_70 b. 10_30 c. 80_100 d. 0_20
   e. 40_60 f. 65_75
5.a. 20 b. 30   6. 6, 9, 12, 15   7. 15, 18_24
8.a. 6_12 b. 15_21 c. 18_24 d. 9_15
9.a. 10, 12, 14, 16 b. 15, 18, 21, 24
   c. 25, 30, 35, 40 d. 50, 60, 70, 80
10.a. 25 cents b. $1 (100 cents) c. $10
11. 12, 15, 18, 21

p7

1.a. 10, 12_16 b. 12, 15_21 c. 10, 15_25
2.a. 12, 16, 27, 39, 23 b. 15, 19, 30, 42, 26
   c. 16, 20, 31, 43, 27 d. 14, 18, 29, 41, 25
3.a.

8	7	15
5	3	8
13	10	23

b.

5	8	13
6	4	10
11	12	23

4.a. 33, 34 b. 99, 100
5.a. 14, 16, 18, 20 b. 21, 24, 27, 30
   c. 70, 80, 90, 100 d. 30, 35, 40, 45
6.a. 3, 6, 9, 12, 15, 18, 21, 24, 27, 30
   b. 2, 4, 6, 8, 10, 12, 14, 16, 18, 20
7. 8 skips of 5

p8

1. 5, 10, 15, 20, 25, 30, 35, 40, 45, 50
2. 15, 20, 25, 30, 35, 40
3.a. 7_17 b. 49_59 c. 20_30 d. 33_43
   e. 26_36 f. 68_78 g. 22_32 h. 41_51
4.a. 50, 60, 70, 80 b. 58, 48, 38, 28
   c. 65, 75, 85, 95
5.a. 54_74 b. 17_37 c. 42_62 d. 28_48
   e. 31_51 f. 73_93

6. 15, 20_30
7.a. 15, 17, 21 b. 37, 39, 41 c. 49, 47, 45
8.a. 10, 30, 35 b. 20, 15, 10, 5
   c. 70, 65, 55 d. 32, 27, 22, 17, 12
9. 42, 46, 48
10.a. 81, 84, 87 b. 74, 77, 80 c. 18, 21, 24
    d. 45, 48, 51

p9

1.a. 45 b. 16 c. 24 d. 48 e. 63
2.a. 7 tens 5 ones 75 b. 8 tens 3 ones 83
   c. 2 tens 6 ones 26 d. 3 tens 9 ones 39
3.a. 36 b. 54 c. 61 d. 48
4.a. 7T, 6O b. 4T, 3O c. 6T9O d. 8T5O
5. 51, 37, 57, 39, 33, 25, 19
6. 9, 11, 15, 17, 21, 23, 25
7. Numbers are all odd.
8.a. 6 b. 7 c. 18 d. 25 e. 32 f. 15
9.a. 13 b. 12 c. 13 d. 35 e. 25 f. 30 g. 26 h. 17

▢ = even numbers

p10

1. apple 2nd, ice cream 3rd, orange 5th, banana 6th, juice bottle 7th
2.a. 28th b. 65th c. 32nd d. 20th e. 100th
   f. 51st g. 44th h. 23rd
3.a. 19th b. 33rd c. 42nd d. 21st e. 49th
   f. 64th
4. Letter c 5. 8th 6. Friday
7. August   8. 25th December
9.a. ones b. tens c. tens d. tens e. tens f. tens
10.a. eighty-seven b. sixty-four c. thirty-nine
    d. fifty-one e. sixty f. forty-eight
11.a. 48, 49, 50, 51 b. 66, 65, 64, 63
    c. 37, 42, 47, 52 d. 65, 70, 75, 80
12.a. 62nd b. 60th c. 41st d. 20th
    e. 46th f. 55th
13.a. 58_62 b. 20_24 c. 56_58 d. 46_50
    e. 72_74 f. 96_100

p11

1. eighty-seven 2. 7 tens 3. 46
4. 7→10→13→16→19→22→25→28→ finish
5.a. 20 b. 30 c. 40 d. 50
6. 89 7. 55_75 8. smaller than 9. 9 x 5
10. 32 11.a. 78 b. 81
12. 45 cents 13.a. $48 b. $63
14. 48, 53, 58, 63, 69, 73
15.a. letter i b. N c. FREE

p12

1.a. 532 b. 368 2.a. 644 b. 571 c. 326
d. 245 3.a. 300 b. 190 c. 91 d. 449
4.a. b. 5. 632, 647, 667, 678, 694
6.a. 3 hundreds 6 tens 5 ones
   b. 2 hundreds 4 tens 2 ones
   c. 3 hundreds 8 tens 7 ones
7.a. 433 b. 615 c. 854 d. 597
8.a. 672 b. 859 c. 220
9. 824 b. 590 c. 386

p13

1.a. b.

hundreds tens ones   hundreds tens ones

2.a. 672 b. 368

3.a. four hundred and fifty-three
  b. two hundred and twenty-eight
  c. one hundred and sixty-seven
  d. four hundred and seventy-nine
  e. five hundred and seventy-three

4.a. 462 b. 646 c. 505

5.a. 635 b. 442 c. 601 d. 862 e. 185

6.a. 6H, 3T, 5O b. 4H, 8T, 7O
  c. 1H, 9T, 2O d. 7H, 0T, 6O

7.a. 525 b. 859 c. 367 d. 428

8.a. 753 b. 921 c. 640 d. 832

9. one thousand

p14

1.a. 452 b. 389 c. 749

2.a. 464 b. 397 c. 814

3.a. 564 b. 906

4.a 500 b. 800 c. 500 d. 400 e. 400 f. 200

5.a. 224 ones b. 145 ones c. 345 ones
  d. 366 ones

6.a. 646 b. 316 c. 809 d. 994 e. 1000

7.a. 381, 567, 649, 837, 838, 946
  b. 249, 386, 387, 411, 519, 549

p15

1.a. 314 b. 442 c. 426 d. 704

2.a. 520 b. 330 c. 470 d. 250

3.a. 4H, 7T,4O b. 3H, 8T, 7O c. 2H, 1T, 2O
  d. 7H, 0T, 8O

4.a. 33 b. 53

5.a. ones b. hundreds c. hundreds d. ones
  e. hundreds f. tens

6.a. 673 b. 732 c. 314 d. 107

7.a. 652 b. 497 c. 608

8.a. 6H, 5T, 3O b. 7H, 0T, 2O c. 5H, 1T, 9O

9.a. 72 tens b. 58 tens

p16

1.a. 800, 900, 1000 b. 750, 850, 950
  c. 601, 501, 401 2.a. 259_459 b. 280_480
  c. 386_586_ d. 724_924 e. 519_719
  f. 669_869 g. 521_721 h. 684_984

3.

		808		816		827		834	
800		810		820		830		840	

4.a. 3H, 2T, 4O b. 6H, 4T, 9O c. 7H, 6T, 5O
  d. 3H, 1T, 7O

5.a. 265 b. 355 6. 11, 13, 15, 17, 19

7.a. 219, 362, 390, 413, 658, 872
  b. 372, 403, 519, 728, 731, 866

8. 497

9.a. 800, 801 b. 601, 602 c. 250, 251
  d. 399, 400

10.a. four hundred and forty-four
  b. seven hundred and eighty-three

p17

1.a. is larger than b. is smaller than

2.a. 705, 715, 725 b. 347, 327, 307
  c. 392, 382, 372

3.a. 599, 600 b. 702, 703 c. 430, 431
  d. 300, 301

4.a. 434 b. 547 5. 749

6.a. 700 b. 700 c. 400 d. 600 e. 400 f. 600

7.a. 140 b. 320 c. 570 d. 210 e. 180 f. 520

8.a. 367 b. 201 c. 586

9.a. 759 b. 532 c. 397 d. 867

10.a. 646 b. 316 c. 809

p18

1.a. odd b. even c. odd d. even e. even f. odd

2.a. 12-even b. 14-even c. 15-odd d.11-odd

3.a. always b. never c. never

4.a. 10 b. 35 5.a. 863 b. 427 c. 861 d. 225

6. odd numbers

7.a. 401, 501, 601 b. 350, 400, 450

8.a. 765 b. 448 c. 137 d. 992

9.a. < b. > c. < d. >

p19

Extension 1. 257 2.a. 695 b. 856 c. 109

3. 653 4.a. 647 b. 838 5. 683

6.a. 700 b. 700 c. 500

7. six hundred and forty-seven

8. 600 + 70 + 8 = 678

9.a. tens b. ones c. hundreds d. tens

10.a. 700, 800, 900 b. 550, 650, 750

11. 873, 664, 532, 458, 416, 219

12.a. 417/817 b. 238/638

13.a. is more than b. is more than

14.a. 374 b. 592 15.a. 15 b. 40

p20

1.a. 85,80,75,70 b.39,42,45,48 c.51, 56, 61,6

2.a.

+	16	5	21
	3	7	10
	19	12	31

b.

+	7	11	18
	5	8	13
	12	19	31

c.

–	16	5	11
	7	3	4
	9	2	7

3.a. 18 b. 52 c. 22 d. 36   4.

5.a. 160 b. 83

6.a. 624/824 b. 265/465

7. Colour 300, 500, 600, 200,400.
  Order 200, 300, 400, 500, 600, 700

8.a. 600 + 70+9= 679 b. 400+10+8=418
  c. 500+30+2=532   d. 700+10+5=715

9.a. > b. > c. < d. >

10.a. 285 b. 638

p21

1.a. ✓ b. 5 c. 5 d. 3 e. 4 f. 5

2.a. 5 b. 1 c. 3 d. 2 e. 4 f. 0

3.a. 15 b. 18 c. 14 d. 16 e. 13 f. 15

4.a. 47 b. 58 c. 81

5.a. 10, 7, 6, 5 b. 13, 10, 9, 8 c. 14, 11, 10, 9
  d. 15, 12, 11, 10

6.a. 13⌐8 b. 61⌐6 c. 6⌐4 d. 10⌐10 e. 8⌐10

7.a. 39 b. 48 c. 78 d. 68 e. 39 f. 88 g. 70 h. 5

8. 12, 14, 17, 18, 15, 13, 19

9. 12, 5, 11, 6, 13, 10, 8 10.a. 30 b. 40 c. 60 d. 5

New Syllabus Mentals and Extension 2, Stage

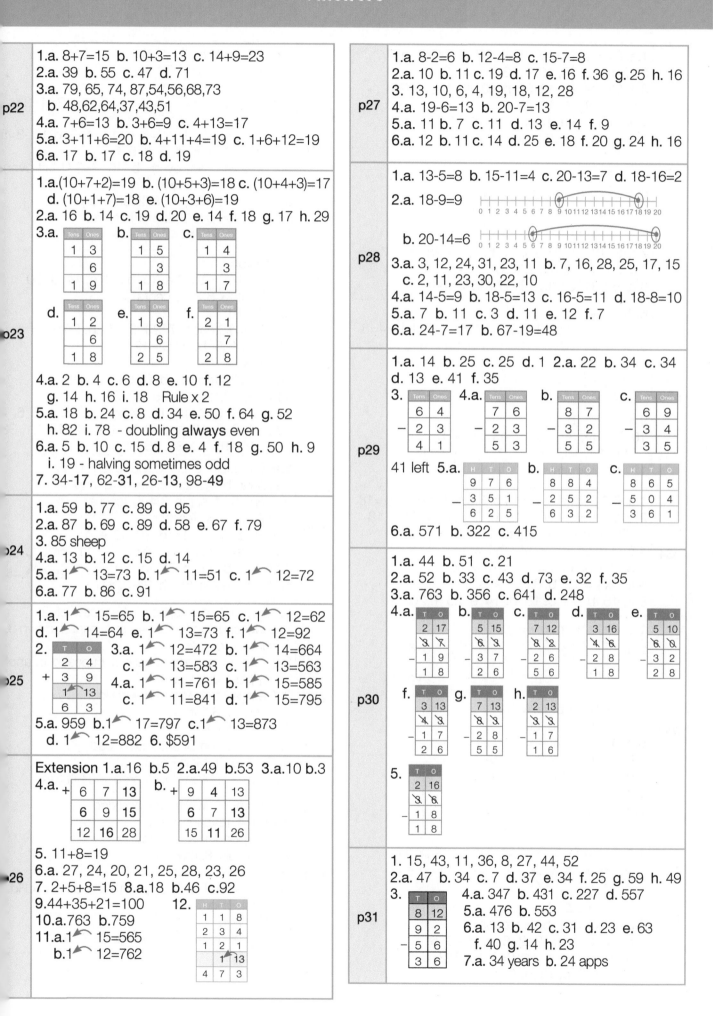

p22

1.a. 8+7=15 b. 10+3=13 c. 14+9=23
2.a. 39 b. 55 c. 47 d. 71
3.a. 79, 65, 74, 87,54,56,68,73
  b. 48,62,64,37,43,51
4.a. 7+6=13 b. 3+6=9 c. 4+13=17
5.a. 3+11+6=20 b. 4+11+4=19 c. 1+6+12=19
6.a. 17 b. 17 c. 18 d. 19

p23

1.a.(10+7+2)=19 b. (10+5+3)=18 c. (10+4+3)=17
  d. (10+1+7)=18 e. (10+3+6)=19
2.a. 16 b. 14 c. 19 d. 20 e. 14 f. 18 g. 17 h. 29

3.a.
Tens	Ones
1	3
	6
1	9

b.
Tens	Ones
1	5
	3
1	8

c.
Tens	Ones
1	4
	3
1	7

d.
Tens	Ones
1	2
	6
1	8

e.
Tens	Ones
1	9
	6
2	5

f.
Tens	Ones
2	1
	7
2	8

4.a. 2 b. 4 c. 6 d. 8 e. 10 f. 12
  g. 14 h. 16 i. 18   Rule x 2
5.a. 18 b. 24 c. 8 d. 34 e. 50 f. 64 g. 52
  h. 82 i. 78 - doubling **always** even
6.a. 5 b. 10 c. 15 d. 8 e. 4 f. 18 g. 50 h. 9
  i. 19 - halving sometimes odd
7. 34-17, 62-31, 26-13, 98-49

p24

1.a. 59 b. 77 c. 89 d. 95
2.a. 87 b. 69 c. 89 d. 58 e. 67 f. 79
3. 85 sheep
4.a. 13 b. 12 c. 15 d. 14
5.a. 1⌢13=73 b. 1⌢11=51 c. 1⌢12=72
6.a. 77 b. 86 c. 91

p25

1.a. 1⌢15=65 b. 1⌢15=65 c. 1⌢12=62
d. 1⌢14=64 e. 1⌢13=73 f. 1⌢12=92
2.
T	O
2	4
+ 3	9
1 ↰	13
6	3

3.a. 1⌢12=472 b. 1⌢14=664
  c. 1⌢13=583 c. 1⌢13=563
4.a. 1⌢11=761 b. 1⌢15=585
  c. 1⌢11=841 d. 1⌢15=795
5.a. 959 b.1⌢17=797 c.1⌢13=873
  d. 1⌢12=882 6. $591

p26

Extension 1.a.16 b.5 2.a.49 b.53 3.a.10 b.3
4.a.
+	6	7	13
	6	9	15
	12	16	28

b.
+	9	4	13
	6	7	13
	15	11	26

5. 11+8=19
6.a. 27, 24, 20, 21, 25, 28, 23, 26
7. 2+5+8=15 8.a.18 b.46 c.92
9.44+35+21=100   12.
H	T	O
1	1	8
2	3	4
1	2	1
	1↰	13
4	7	3

10.a.763 b.759
11.a.1⌢15=565
  b.1⌢12=762

p27

1.a. 8-2=6 b. 12-4=8 c. 15-7=8
2.a. 10 b. 11 c. 19 d. 17 e. 16 f. 36 g. 25 h. 16
3. 13, 10, 6, 4, 19, 18, 12, 28
4.a. 19-6=13 b. 20-7=13
5.a. 11 b. 7 c. 11 d. 13 e. 14 f. 9
6.a. 12 b. 11 c. 14 d. 25 e. 18 f. 20 g. 24 h. 16

p28

1.a. 13-5=8 b. 15-11=4 c. 20-13=7 d. 18-16=2
2.a. 18-9=9 [number line 0–20]
  b. 20-14=6 [number line 0–20]
3.a. 3, 12, 24, 31, 23, 11 b. 7, 16, 28, 25, 17, 15
  c. 2, 11, 23, 30, 22, 10
4.a. 14-5=9 b. 18-5=13 c. 16-5=11 d. 18-8=10
5.a. 7 b. 11 c. 3 d. 11 e. 12 f. 7
6.a. 24-7=17 b. 67-19=48

p29

1.a. 14 b. 25 c. 25 d. 1 2.a. 22 b. 34 c. 34
d. 13 e. 41 f. 35

3.
Tens	Ones
6	4
− 2	3
4	1

4.a.
Tens	Ones
7	6
− 2	3
5	3

b.
Tens	Ones
8	7
− 3	2
5	5

c.
Tens	Ones
6	9
− 3	4
3	5

41 left 5.a.
H	T	O
9	7	6
− 3	5	1
6	2	5

b.
H	T	O
8	8	4
− 2	5	2
6	3	2

c.
H	T	O
8	6	5
− 5	0	4
3	6	1

6.a. 571 b. 322 c. 415

p30

1.a. 44 b. 51 c. 21
2.a. 52 b. 33 c. 43 d. 73 e. 32 f. 35
3.a. 763 b. 356 c. 641 d. 248
4.a.
T	O
2	17
3̶	7̶
− 1	9
1	8

b.
T	O
5	15
6̶	3̶
− 3	7
2	6

c.
T	O
7	12
8̶	2̶
− 2	6
5	6

d.
T	O
3	16
4̶	6̶
− 2	8
1	8

e.
T	O
5	10
6̶	0̶
− 3	2
2	8

f.
T	O
3	13
4̶	3̶
− 1	7
2	6

g.
T	O
7	13
8̶	3̶
− 2	8
5	5

h.
T	O
2	13
3̶	3̶
− 1	7
1	6

5.
T	O
2	16
3̶	6̶
− 1	8
1	8

p31

1. 15, 43, 11, 36, 8, 27, 44, 52
2.a. 47 b. 34 c. 7 d. 37 e. 34 f. 25 g. 59 h. 49
3.
T	O
8	12
9	2̶
− 5	6
3	6

4.a. 347 b. 431 c. 227 d. 557
5.a. 476 b. 553
6.a. 13 b. 42 c. 31 d. 23 e. 63
  f. 40 g. 14 h. 23
7.a. 34 years b. 24 apps

p32

1.a. Example b. 15/15 c. 7/7 d. 44/44 e. 7/7
f. 13/13 2. 18, 15, 9, 13, 16, 20, 8, 19
3.a. 32, 39, 26, 19, 24 b. 33, 40, 27, 20, 25
  c. 31, 38, 25, 18, 23
4.

T	O
	14
3̸	4̸
− 1	6
1	8

5.a. 14+13 b. 15/15
  c. 39/39 d. 49/49

6.a. +

4	8	12
9	7	16
13	15	28

b. −

18	12	6
7	5	2
11	7	4

7.a. 3, 12, 24, 31, 23, 11 b. 7, 16, 28, 35, 27, 15
  c. 2, 11, 23, 30, 22, 10
8.a. 62-31=31 b. 12+17+35 = $64

p33

Extension
1.17-5=12 2.a.14 b.39 3.17-13=4 4.12-4=8
5.

Tens	Ones
6	7
− 3	4
3	3

6.

H	T	O
7	3	6
− 4	1	5
3	2	1

7.a. 441 b. 511
8.a. 338 b. 525
  c. 446

9.a. 11/11 b. 25/25
10. 29, 44, 36, 33, 11. −

24	11	13
18	5	13
6	6	0

  20, 31, 13, 38
12. 13 kilometres

p34

1.a. 7,7-2 rows of 7 = 14 b. 6,6,6-3 rows of 6 =18
2.a. 3 groups of 6 = 18 b. 3 groups of 6 = 18
3. Teacher - 2 groups of 10 = 20
4.a. 2 rows of 7 = 14 / 2x7 = 14
  b. 3 rows of 6 = 18 / 3x6 = 18
5.a. 3x4 = 12 b. 3x3 = 9
6.a. 16 b. 15 c. 18 d. 14 e. 25 f. 20

p35

1.a. 5x3=15 b. 5x4=20
2.a.
0 1 2 3 4 5 6 7 8 9 10 11 12 13 14 15 16 17 18 19 20 3x6=18
  b.
0 1 2 3 4 5 6 7 8 9 10 11 12 13 14 15 16 17 18 19 20 2x9=18
3.a. 3x6=18 b. 4x4=16
4.a. 12 b. 14 c. 20 d. 18
5.a. 4 groups of 4 = 16, 4x4 = 16
  b. 3 groups of 5 = 15, 3x5 = 15
  c. 2 rows of 7 = 14, 2x7 = 14
6. 5x3 = 15
7.a. 12 b. 12 c. 20 d. 20
8. 4 x $5 = $20

p36

1.a. $4 each b. 2 cakes each c. 4 pegs
2. ▲▲▲▲▲▲ 21 divided into 3 = 7
△△△△△▲
△△△▲▲▲
    ▲▲▲
3.a.two groups b.six groups
4.a. 12÷3=4 b. 12÷2=6 c. 15÷3=5
  d. 20÷10=2 e. 14÷2=7 f. 12÷2=6
5.a. 4 b. 5 c. 10 d. 6 e. 5 f. 6

p37

1.a. 16÷4=4 b. 15÷3=5
2.a.
0 1 2 3 4 5 6 7 8 9 10 11 12 13 14 15 16 17 18 19 20 14÷2=7
  b.
0 1 2 3 4 5 6 7 8 9 10 11 12 13 14 15 16 17 18 19 20 12÷4=3
3.a. 12÷3=4 b. 15÷5=3 c. 12÷4=3 d.15÷3=5
4.a. 9 b. 7 c. 6 d. 6 e. 5 f. 7
5.a. 9÷2=4 (1 left over) b. 10÷3=3 (1 left over)
c. 17÷3=5 (2 left over)
6.a. 9 (0 left over) b. 3 (2 left over)
  c. 5 (1 left over) d. 3 (1 left over)
7.a. 15÷3= $5 b. 40÷10= $4

p38

Extension
1. 5 2. 4x4 = 16 3.a. 15 b. 24 c. 14 d. 30
4. 5 cents x 8 = 40 cents
5. 8x2=16
6. 18÷3=$6 each 7. 20÷2=10 b. 25÷5=5
8.a. 20÷4=5 b. 24÷2=12
9. 16÷4=4
10.a. 2 (2 left over) b. 6 (1 left over)
11.a. 5, 10, 15, 20, 25, 30, 35
  b. 2, 4, 6, 8, 10, 12, 14 c. 1, 2, 3, 4, 5, 6, 7
12.a. 4, 6, 8, 12, 14, 22 b. 6, 9, 12, 18, 21, 33
  c. 10, 15, 20, 30, 35, 55

p39

1.a. E5 b. D4 c. B4 d. C8 e. C1 f. A3
2.a. pear b. orange c. pencil d. cupcake
e. umbrella f. apple 3/4/5. Teacher
6. balloon 7/8. Teacher
9.a. 28 b. 15 c. 15 d. 30, 32 e. 4
10.a. threes b. tens c. fives 11. (26) (30)
12.a. 1st b. 4th c. 7th d. 5th   (40)
e. 3rd f. 2nd g. 6th h. 9th i. 8th (25) (45)

p40

1. forward 2 spaces, down 4 spaces, left 2
  spaces, down 2, right 4, up 4, right 2, down 3,
  right 2, down 3.
2.a. orange b. pear c. pear d. cupcake e. app.
  f. apple and cupcake
3. George St 4. Main Rd and Boundary St
5. Short St 6. Pitt St
7. church/library
8. Corner Short St and Main Road
9. George St, Main Road
10. yes 11. Main Rd, George and Pitt Sts

p41

1. windmill 2. water tank and dog
3. dog 4. teacher 5. car
6. duckpond, man and tractor
7. 5 animals 8. man
9. teacher - chemist
10. Patterson Rd, Thompson Rd and Fairfax Rd
11. Post Office
12. Owl Ave
13. corner of Hawk St and Fairfax Road

New Syllabus Mentals and Extension 2, Stage C

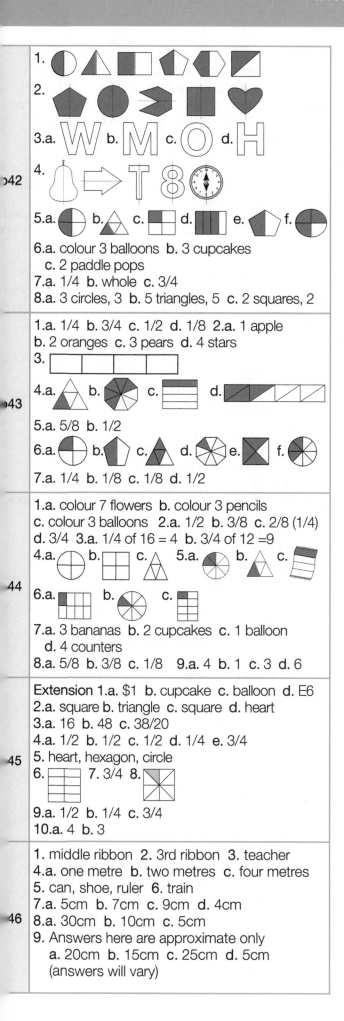

p42

1.
2.
3.a. W b. M c. O d. H
4.
5.a. b. c. d. e. f.
6.a. colour 3 balloons b. 3 cupcakes
  c. 2 paddle pops
7.a. 1/4 b. whole c. 3/4
8.a. 3 circles, 3 b. 5 triangles, 5 c. 2 squares, 2

p43

1.a. 1/4 b. 3/4 c. 1/2 d. 1/8 2.a. 1 apple
b. 2 oranges c. 3 pears d. 4 stars
3.
4.a. b. c. d.
5.a. 5/8 b. 1/2
6.a. b. c. d. e. f.
7.a. 1/4 b. 1/8 c. 1/8 d. 1/2

p44

1.a. colour 7 flowers b. colour 3 pencils
c. colour 3 balloons 2.a. 1/2 b. 3/8 c. 2/8 (1/4)
d. 3/4 3.a. 1/4 of 16 = 4 b. 3/4 of 12 =9
4.a. b. c. 5.a. b. c.
6.a. b. c.
7.a. 3 bananas b. 2 cupcakes c. 1 balloon
  d. 4 counters
8.a. 5/8 b. 3/8 c. 1/8 9.a. 4 b. 1 c. 3 d. 6

p45

Extension 1.a. $1 b. cupcake c. balloon d. E6
2.a. square b. triangle c. square d. heart
3.a. 16 b. 48 c. 38/20
4.a. 1/2 b. 1/2 c. 1/2 d. 1/4 e. 3/4
5. heart, hexagon, circle
6.   7. 3/4 8.
9.a. 1/2 b. 1/4 c. 3/4
10.a. 4 b. 3

p46

1. middle ribbon 2. 3rd ribbon 3. teacher
4.a. one metre b. two metres c. four metres
5. can, shoe, ruler 6. train
7.a. 5cm b. 7cm c. 9cm d. 4cm
8.a. 30cm b. 10cm c. 5cm
9. Answers here are approximate only
  a. 20cm b. 15cm c. 25cm d. 5cm
  (answers will vary)

p47

1. Exercise is a physical activity. Answers will
   vary. Answers given are approximate.
   a. 24cm b. 25cm c. 22cm d. 24cm
   e. 15cm f. 11cm g. 24cm h. 18cm
2. Answers will also vary a-f. teacher
3.a. 33cm b. 18cm (lengths will vary)
4.a. 7cm b. 5cm c. 9cm
5.a. 10cm b. 13cm c. 18cm d. 14cm

p48

1.   2.a. broken line
b. parallel lines c. joining lines d. curved lines
e. crossed lines 3. a and c
4.a. b. c. 5.a. triangle
   b. square
   c. hexagon
d. rhombus e. pentagon f. trapezium
g. octagon h. semi-circle 6. b, d and f
7. 3 hexagon, pentagon, octagon

p49

1.a. 3 edges, 3 vertices b. c and d same as a
2. yes 3. a, b, c and d 4 edges, 4 vertices
4. yes 5. b only 6. hexagons a, b, d and f
7.a. b. c. d.
8. Colour a, c, e and f - octagons

p50

1. Colour c and e 2.a. rhombus b. trapezium
3. yes 4. yes
5. triangle 6. circle
7. a and b red, d and f c. trapezium d. rhombus
   yellow, c and e blue
8.a.
   b.   9. colour b and c
      10. rhombus
      11. pentagon

p51

Extension 1. yes 2. 100cm 3. true 4. 12cm
5. 25cm 6. true 7. 8cm 8. zig zag line
9.a. square b. circle c. hexagon 10. 4 sides
11. 7 edges, 7 vertices 12.a. c.
13. colour a, b, d and f
14.a. rhombus b. trapezium
15.a. 300cm 11. 250cm

p52

1.a. b. c. d.
2.a. slid along b. turned around c. flipped over
3. AMXO 4.a. b. c. d.
5.a. quarter turn clockwise
   b. quarter turn anticlockwise
   c. full turn clockwise 6. 4 turns 7. 2 turns

p53

1.colour a, c, d and e 2. colour c
3. c, d, e, a, b
4.a. 20 b. 23 c. 25 Colour b
5. Australia
6.a. 15 squares b. 10 triangles c. 16 hexagons

p54

1.a. pyramid b. cube c. cylinder d. cone
   e. sphere f. rectangular prism
2.a. cone b. cylinder c. sphere d. cube
   e. cylinder (a coin has depth on sides)
3.a. 5 face, 5 vertices, 5 edges
   b. 3 faces, 2 vertices, 3 edges
4.a. sphere b. cube c. hexagonal prism
   d. cylinder e. cone f. triangular prism
5.a. rectangular prism b. triangular prism c. cube
6. balloon, marble, glass, rolling pin, traffic cone

p55

1. a matches f, b matches h, c matches e,
   d matches g
2.a. pyramid b. cylinder c. cube d. cone
3.a. rectangular prism b. cylinder c. cone
   d. hexagonal prism
4.a. △ b. ▢ c. ▽ d. ▢   5. 8 edges

p56

1.a. hexagonal pyramid b. rectangular pyramid
   c. triangular pyramid d. square pyramid
2. brick, coin, dice
3.a. [triangular prism]   b. [cylinder]   c. [rectangular prism]

   cylinder   rectangular prism   triangular prism
4.a. pyramid b. cube 5. 6 faces 6. cone
7. pentagonal prism 8. yes 9. one
10. cone and semi-circle
11.a. hexagonal prism b. cylinder
12. [quarter circle shape]

p57

1.a. 10 cubes b. 14 cubes 2. a, b, d
3.a. 30 blocks b. 22 blocks c. 31 blocks
4. 1st b, 2nd a, 3rd c
5.a. length 4, height 6, width 1
   b. length 3, height 6, width 1
6. colour a blocks
7.a. 4x6x1=24 blocks b. 3x6x1=18 blocks
8.a. 30 blocks b. 32 blocks
-9. b 10. yes

p58

1. potato 2. volume 3. a,b,c,d
4. pumpkin, football, plasticine, banana
5. cup and saucer, tissue box, bucket
6. jug 7. teacher approx.8-10
8.a. teacher approx. 9 to 11
   b. teacher approx. 4 to 6.

p59

1.a. 9 litres b. 2 litres c. 300 litres
   d. 60 litres e. 1500 litres
2. more than, teacher - kettle, milk bottle,
   juice bottle, less than, teacher - soft drink can,
   cup, mug, glass
3. can, glass, paint tin, bucket, tissue box
4.a. 11 jugs b. 35 cups full c. 16 pots
5. jug
6. 1st kettle, 2nd orange juice, 3rd can,
   4th cup and saucer, 5th glass,
   6th medicine glass, 7th thimble

p60

1.a. 4th b. 2nd c. 1st d. 3rd e. 5th f. 6th
2.a. tennis ball b. empty can c. kiwi fruit
   d. tooth brush e. fork f. ruler
3.a. cup with saucer b. orange c. margarine
   d. orange juice e. boot f. tomato sauce
4.a. up ↑ b. up ↑ c. down ↓ d. up ↑
5. apple, dice, glass

p61

1.a. banana b. sugar c. sauce bottle d. orange
   e. cup f. bread
2.a. [balance image] b. [balance image] c. [balance image] d. [balance image] answers may vary
3.a. more than a kilogram b. about a kilogram
   c. less than a kilogram d. more than a kilogram
   e. more than a kilogram f. less than a kilogram
4. Teacher - suggestions -
   lighter - eggs, scissors, pieces of fruit
   heavier - milk, bottle, juice bottle, soft drink,
   bottle
5. 1st scissors, 2nd can, 3rd peanut butter,
   4th brick, 5th full kettle

p62

Extension 1. b. larger volume
2. balloon, can 3. stapler 4. banana
5. pumpkin, orange juice 6. jug
7.a. 22 b. 26 8. balloon
9. lightest - 1st duster, 2nd pencil case, 3rd book
   4th sticky tape
10. 4x3x2=24 blocks
11. right tray - down
12. 14 kilograms

p63

1. 1st Monday, 2nd Tuesday, 3rd Wednesday,
   4th Thursday, 5th Friday, 6th Saturday
2. November 30 days, August 31 days,
   March 31 days, January 31 days, April,
   30 days, September 30 days
3. 7 months   4.a. Spring b. Autumn
5. June, July, August 6. 92 days
7.a. May-July b. December - February
   c. July-September
8. 92 days 9. Thursday 1st April
10. Sunday 25th April 11. Saturday
12. 3rd and 4th 13. Autumn
14. 14 days 15. 4 months
16. Wednesday 17. 4 weekends

p64

1. Tuesday 2. 25th and 26th
3. Friday 1st July 4. Yes
5. Saturday 11th, Sunday 12th, Monday 13th
6. April, September, November 7. Winter
8. Thursday 9. Saturday 10. 3rd and 4th
11. Wednesday 31st May
12. 5 Saturdays 13. 26th and 27th
14. 92 days
15. Yes/No teacher

New Syllabus Mentals and Extension 2, Stage

Answers

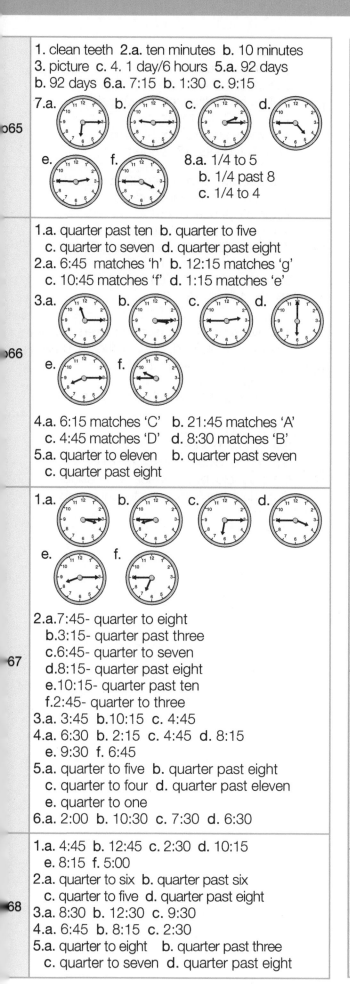

p65

1. clean teeth 2.a. ten minutes b. 10 minutes
3. picture c. 4. 1 day/6 hours 5.a. 92 days
b. 92 days 6.a. 7:15 b. 1:30 c. 9:15
7.a. b. c. d.
e. f. 8.a. 1/4 to 5
   b. 1/4 past 8
   c. 1/4 to 4

p66

1.a. quarter past ten b. quarter to five
   c. quarter to seven d. quarter past eight
2.a. 6:45 matches 'h' b. 12:15 matches 'g'
   c. 10:45 matches 'f' d. 1:15 matches 'e'
3.a. b. c. d.
e. f.
4.a. 6:15 matches 'C' b. 21:45 matches 'A'
   c. 4:45 matches 'D' d. 8:30 matches 'B'
5.a. quarter to eleven b. quarter past seven
   c. quarter past eight

p67

1.a. b. c. d.
e. f.
2.a. 7:45- quarter to eight
   b. 3:15- quarter past three
   c. 6:45- quarter to seven
   d. 8:15- quarter past eight
   e. 10:15- quarter past ten
   f. 2:45- quarter to three
3.a. 3:45 b. 10:15 c. 4:45
4.a. 6:30 b. 2:15 c. 4:45 d. 8:15
   e. 9:30 f. 6:45
5.a. quarter to five b. quarter past eight
   c. quarter to four d. quarter past eleven
   e. quarter to one
6.a. 2:00 b. 10:30 c. 7:30 d. 6:30

p68

1.a. 4:45 b. 12:45 c. 2:30 d. 10:15
   e. 8:15 f. 5:00
2.a. quarter to six b. quarter past six
   c. quarter to five d. quarter past eight
3.a. 8:30 b. 12:30 c. 9:30
4.a. 6:45 b. 8:15 c. 2:30
5.a. quarter to eight b. quarter past three
   c. quarter to seven d. quarter past eight

p68

6.a. b. c.
d. e. f.
7. Teacher/parent - 6:30

p69

Extension 1. 30 days 2. August 3. 25th April
4. March, April, May 5. half an hour
6. eight o'clock 7. 3:30
8. quarter past three
9. 10. 6:15 11. 9:15 12. half past three
   13. quarter to three 14. 60 minutes
   15. 15 minutes 16. 8:30 (last clock)
   17. Teacher/parent 18. 45 minutes
19.

p70

1.a. ten cents b. fifty cents c. one dollar
   d. five cents
2. 1st $2, 2nd $1, 3rd 50c. 4th 20c, 5th 10c,
   6th 5c
3.a. $2.75 b. $3.70 c. $1.35 d. $1.60
4.a. $2+$2+20c+10c+5c
   b. $2+$1+50c+20c+5c
   c. $1+$1+20c+10c
5.a. $16 b. $10 c. $36
6.a. 95c b. 90c c. 50c d. 50c

p71

1.a. one dollar b. twenty cents c. fifty cents
2.a. 60c b. 30c c. 65c d. 65c e. $1 f. 85c
3.a. $3.25 b. $2.90 c. $3.25
4.a. $3.85 b. $3.75 c. $4.35 d. $4
5.a. $1 b. 25c c. 10c d. 75c e. 35c f. 90c
6.a. is equal to b. not equal to

p72

1.a. fifty dollars b. five dollars c. ten dollars
   d. one hundred dollars e. twenty dollars
2.a. $5, $10, $20, $50, $100
3.a. 2 x $5 b. 10 x $5 c. 4 x $5
4.a. 5 x $10 b. 10 x $10 c. 2 x $10
5.a. five dollars b. fifty dollars c. fifty cents
   d. twenty dollars e. one dollar f. twenty cents
   g. two dollars
6.a. $151.50 b. $33.35
7. $10+$15=$25

p73

1.a. $17.05 b. $78.75 c. $53.60
2.a. $38.50 b. $80.95 c. $34.85
3.a. 1st $50, 2nd $20, 3rd $10, 4th $5, 5th $2,
   6th 50c, 7th 20c
4.a. $65 b. $80
5.a. $10+$5+$2+$1+$1+50c+20c+20c+5c
6.a. $90 b. $75

Answers

p74
1.a. $5.70 b. $37.70 c. $63.20
2.a. $5+$5+$2+$2+50c
 b. $20+$5+$5+$1+$1+50c+10c
3.a. $37.90 b. $19.50
4.a. $25.75 b. $125.70
5.a. $10 b. $25 c. $5 d. $15 e. $50 f. $20
6. 7. icecream, sandwich, can of soft drink
8. 12 years old
9. yes

p75
Extension
1. 20c 2. $1 3. 5x5c
4. $1.85 5. 10 cents b. 25 coins
7.a. 65c b. 85c c. 60c
8. is equal to
9. five dollars
10.a. blue b. red c. green d. yellow
11. $20 12. 10x$10
13. $14.70 14. $20.25
15. yes 16. 5c, 10c, 20c, 50c, $1, $2
17. one hundred dollars

p76
1. banana 2. 7 3. grapes 4. 4
5. orange, pear 6. 7 7. 6
8. student 9. 38 10. cat
11. 7 12. guinea pig
13. 5 14. 6 15. 4 16. student
17. 38 18. student

p77
1. blue 12, yellow 8, green 11, black 6, orange 7, red 14
2. red 3. 12 4. black 5. blue 6. 4
7. 4 8. 58 9. student 10. English
11. 4 12. 2 13. Music
14. Maths and PE 15. 5 16. 6
17. 29 students 18. student

p78
1.a. biscuits 16 b. sauce 23 c. flour 18
 d. jam 15 e. peanut butter 18
2. tomato sauce 3. jam
4. flour and peanut butter 5. 8 6. student
7. Tallies - Rhani 12, Eli 8, Jon 8, Paris 9, Josie 10, Samira 11, Li 13, Kim 7
8. 13 9. 10 10. Li 11. Kim 12. 3
13. 55 14. 23 15. 78

p79
1.a. likely/unlikely - personal answers will vary
 b. likely c. likely d. likely e. likely f. unlikely
2. a, b and d 3. student activity
4. student record
5, 6, 7, 8, 9, 10 - student 11. no 12. no

p80
1.a. 5 b. B c. X d. 2
2.a. yellow b. blue
3.a. red b. blue 4. possible 5. B
6.a. possible b. impossible c. possible
7. student activity a, b, c student record
 d. no

Notes

New Syllabus Mentals and Extension 2, Stage